YAGA

ALSO BY KAT SANDLER

Mustard
Punch Up
BANG BANG

YAGA
KAT SANDLER

PLAYWRIGHTS CANADA PRESS
TORONTO

Playwrights Canada Press
202-269 Richmond St. w., Toronto, ON, M5V 1X1
416.703.0013 | info@playwrightscanada.com | www.playwrightscanada.com

LIBRARY AND ARCHIVES CANADA CATALOGUING IN PUBLICATION
Title: Yaga / Kat Sandler.
Names: Sandler, Kat, author.
Description: A play.
Identifiers: Canadiana (print) 20220157987 | Canadiana (ebook) 20220158002
  | ISBN 9780369101655 (softcover) | ISBN 9780369101662 (PDF)
  | ISBN 9780369101679 (HTML)
Classification: LCC PS8637.A5455 Y34 2022 | DDC C812/.6—dc23

Playwrights Canada Press operates on land which is the ancestral home of the Anishinaabe Nations (Ojibwe / Chippewa, Odawa, Potawatomi, Algonquin, Saulteaux, Nipissing, and Mississauga), the Wendat, and the members of the Haudenosaunee Confederacy (Mohawk, Oneida, Onondaga, Cayuga, Seneca, and Tuscarora), as well as Metis and Inuit peoples. It always was and always will be Indigenous land.

We acknowledge the financial support of the Canada Council for the Arts, the Ontario Arts Council (OAC), Ontario Creates, and the Government of Canada for our publishing activities.

For wise, witchy, powerful women everywhere.
(But especially my mom, Ann.)

Yaga was developed and first produced by Tarragon Theatre, Toronto, from September 17 to October 27, 2019, with the following cast and creative team:

Actors: Claire Armstrong, Will Greenblatt, and Seana McKenna

Director: Kat Sandler
Set and Costume Design: Joanna Yu
Lighting Design: Jennifer Lennon
Sound Design: Chris Ross-Ewart
Dramaturg: Joanna Falck
Fight Director: Simon Fon
Stage Manager: Sarah Miller
Apprentice Stage Manager: Jaimee Hall
Consulting Dramaturg: Jill Harper
Dialect Coach: Victor Mishalow

SETTING

Fog and smoke. Dust motes dance in the light. A raised platform of wooden planks sits on a dirt floor surrounded by upright birch stalks—a vast and magical forest. Chicken feathers and piles of dirt litter the edges of the stage. A table. Mismatched chairs. There's something in the air: tension, power, wickedness, but also good. Through lights, sound, and simple furniture rearrangement, the space should evoke a woodsy cabin, a police station, a diner, a dorm room, coffee shop, motel, etc. Props and costumes can be hung in the trees on hooks or shelves.

TRANSITIONS

Wherever possible, transition seamlessly into the next scene, shifting lighting and sound with no blackout between scenes. When actors are not in a scene, they remain on stage. Yaga can shift some of the elements around in her monologues too, in effect, "setting the stage" for us and Rapp.

PUNCTUATION

A forward slash (/) marks the point in a character's line where the next character begins speaking, causing an overlap of speech. The first character continues speaking until they run out of text or feel cut off by the next line.

An asterisk (*) at the end of a line is the cue for a character to speak who has an asterisk at the beginning of their line, even though on the page a line or more of dialogue may separate the first character's lines from the response of the second. The lines will overlap.

When words appear in CAPS, it doesn't necessarily mean that they should be yelled, but just given a certain intensity.

When lines appear in (brackets) within another line, the in-bracket character "tucks" their dialogue into the line, usually during a breath, in VERY quick succession—there's no overlap.

An ellipsis (. . .) indicates a character thinking or searching for a response. They usually indicate a *slight* hesitation, and are not meant as long pauses or beats or trail-offs.

PACE

Pick it up.

CHARACTERS

Woman A Plays the Following Roles:
YAGA: a witch; old, ugly, evil, or so they say
KATHERINE YAZOV: a university professor in her sixties
GEENA SANDESON: Lily's mother; a diner owner in her fifties
ELENA: a naturopath in her nineties
JANICE: a shy trucker in her forties
STAFF SARGENT SIDLE: in her sixties

Woman B Plays the Following Roles:
DETECTIVE CARSON: in her thirties
TRULY: a neighbour in her forties
PAMELA RILEY: Henry's ex-girlfriend, a student in her twenties
LILY SANDESON: a waitress, Geena's daughter, fifteen
ANNA: in her thirties
DEPUTY MURPHY: in her thirties

Man Plays the Following Roles:
CHARLIE RAPP: a private investigator in his late twenties
HENRY KALLES: a student in his early twenties

ACT ONE

YOU SAY

Darkness. Lights fade up on YAGA *as she emerges from the woods. An eerie, ancient soundscape, women's voices. She speaks with a slight Eastern European accent.*

YAGA: Let's start with what you say.

You say I am *old*, old as the earth, as wicked as the night, and as wise and powerful as the sea, that I was there at the beginning of time to ring in the first sun, the first monster, the first man.

You say I am *ugly*, that I have a nose like a gargoyle, that my eyes are made of embers burning deep in sockets of dry black pitch, my teeth are gnashing iron, my spittle dark, wet blood that drips down to the bristles at my chin, and that if you die screaming, I am the last thing you see.

Not a pretty picture, huh?

You say I live alone in the woods, in a hut that stands on chicken feet, surrounded by a fence made of skulls, with one post empty, always, for my next victim. You say there is no way in unless it is already too late, for the hut reveals its door only to me, when I speak the words.

You say I fly in a mortar and pestle, sweeping a broom behind me to cover my tracks, eating naughty children, their fingers, legs, and guts, their earlobes, and, best of all, their *bones*, grinding them till they are fine as dust and sprinkle them on my vegetables.

But the thing that really gets me is this:

You say that I am lonely, that no one will love me, that no one will *fuck* me, for my body is barren, my breasts ancient, lifeless sacks that drag through the dirt at my feet, my sex as dry as sand and twice as dusty, a ring of teeth around a gaping, bloodless gash. You say that I have taken and will take no lovers, and this, this must be true, for who could love such a *beast*, such a *thing* as I am?

But you also say I am the grandmother of the devil . . .

So someone must have.

You say these things as if I cannot hear them.
You say these things as if there's nothing more.
You say these things and now it's time to *listen*.

> *She leans forward impossibly slowly, as if to tell us a secret, suddenly, terrifying:*

ARE YOU LISTENING?

> *Blackout.*

LIZARD

Lights snap up. HENRY *and* KATHERINE *in* HENRY's *dorm room.*

HENRY: Sorry about the mess.

KATHERINE: Oh, it's not that bad—my kid was a disaster.

HENRY: I had another interview.

KATHERINE: Why didn't you interview *me* here?

HENRY: Oh, it didn't seem . . . appropriate.

KATHERINE picks up a Pokémon toque.

KATHERINE: This is *yours*?

HENRY: *(putting it on)* Hey! My nephew got it for me. I like it. What, you don't like Pokémon?

KATHERINE: *(looking around)* You have your own room.

HENRY: Yeah, my mother thought it was important to have my own space cuz last year my roommate turned out to be kind of, um, slutty and just like . . . fucked on everything. (**KATHERINE:** Oh.) Sorry.

KATHERINE: Sorry for what?

HENRY: Saying fuck.

KATHERINE: That's all right, I've heard it before.

KATHERINE spots something on a table.

HENRY: That's / uh . . .

KATHERINE: I know what pot looks like. I assume you acquired it legally. Should we smoke it?

HENRY: *(surprised)* Oh . . . ! I . . . yeah, totally. I can / roll—

KATHERINE: I can roll my own joint, thank you very much. *(starts to roll a joint)* I lived through the '70s, you know.

HENRY: Right.

KATHERINE: Were you jealous?

HENRY: Of the '70s?

KATHERINE: Of all the fucking.

HENRY: *(beat)* No. Oh, God, no. Because I also have so much . . . sex . . . *lots* of sex . . . so . . .

KATHERINE: Good for you.

HENRY: On *beds*, though.

KATHERINE: A traditionalist.

HENRY: No . . . I mean, people pretend that it's like, hot and exciting, to have sex on stuff like . . . desks—

KATHERINE: Desks.

HENRY: Yeah, but the best sex *I've* ever had is on beds, good, old-fashioned mattress-covered beds. I'm so sorry.

KATHERINE: Why?

HENRY: Oh, well, you know, because you're not worried about sharp corners, like, digging into your ribs, or spinny office chairs throwing your rhythm off / and—

KATHERINE: No, why are you sorry?

HENRY: *(embarrassed)* Oh. I don't know—I'm sorry—we don't have to talk about / this . . .

KATHERINE: I don't want to alarm you, Henry,*

HENRY: Sorry . . .

KATHERINE: *but *I've had sex.*

HENRY: Yeah, totally. I / know that.

KATHERINE: A lot.

HENRY: Okay.

KATHERINE: A lot more than you.

HENRY: Yeah, that's fine.

KATHERINE: Fine?

HENRY: I mean, good, that's good for you.

KATHERINE: Well, thanks very much.

HENRY: No, no, sorry, I'm sorry, I know, of course you have, because you're . . .

Beat.

KATHERINE: I'm . . . ?

HENRY: Old . . . er. *(beat)* A bit.

KATHERINE: A lot.

HENRY: Right, so just by virtue of the time you've had on earth to be having sex, you've had more than me.

KATHERINE: Well, that, yes, and I like sex.

HENRY: Good.

KATHERINE: A lot, (HENRY: Great!) so I've had it a *lot*, with *lots* of people.

HENRY: Totally. / Totally.

KATHERINE: It's not a thing to be precious about.

HENRY: I'm not . . . / *precious.*

KATHERINE: Good / good.

HENRY: Totally.

KATHERINE: We're animals. (HENRY: Yeah.) Beasts.

HENRY: "The beast with two backs." (KATHERINE: Very good.) Me too.

KATHERINE: You what?

HENRY: I like sex.

KATHERINE: Good. (HENRY: Yeah.) I happen to like desks. Incidentally.

HENRY: What?

KATHERINE: *Fucking* on desks. The power dynamic, you know—*

HENRY: *(intrigued)* Yeah . . .

KATHERINE: *—bending someone over feels . . . primal.

HENRY: . . . totally.

KATHERINE: And sometimes it's good to be pushed up against something solid. *(HENRY coughs.)* Am I making you uncomfortable?

HENRY: *(awkward high laugh)* No. No. We're just having a professional conversation. We're professionals. Or . . . would you call us colleagues?

KATHERINE: Student is what I would call you.

HENRY: Yeah. I guess that's what I'd be. But not *your* student.

KATHERINE: No. So where's *your* desk? *(beat)* Oh, look at your face.

HENRY: What?

KATHERINE: You're white!

HENRY: No, I'm / not . . .

KATHERINE: I'm so sorry, I'm kidding, I just couldn't stop.

HENRY: It's / fine.

KATHERINE: Look at you! You're terrified!

HENRY: No. Actually, I'm not / at all.

KATHERINE: "Where's your desk?" / HAH!*

HENRY: *(nervous laugh)* Yeah. Yeah.

KATHERINE: *I'm so sorry, I just thought you had a sense of humour.

HENRY: I *do.*

KATHERINE: You don't find this funny?

HENRY: No, I do, it's / *totally hilarious.*

KATHERINE: Because me trying to seduce you would be *totally* inappropriate.

HENRY: *Totally.*

> *They laugh.*

KATHERINE: Do you have anything to drink?

> *Beat.*

HENRY: To drink? Yeah, I think I have some whisky . . .

> *He gets a bottle.*

KATHERINE: Well for God's sake, let's get the whisky out before you die of shock because someone your mother's age said they still enjoy sex.

HENRY: You're older than my mother. So.

KATHERINE: How old do you think I am?

HENRY: Oh, no. No thank you. Pleading the fifth.

KATHERINE: Wise beyond your years.

HENRY: You know, I always thought when people said that, they were saying, "Wash behind your ears."

KATHERINE: Cute.

Beat.

HENRY: So . . . do you want to see it?

KATHERINE: That's why I'm here, isn't it? Your great discovery?

HENRY: Yeah, I just . . . because I know you teach about bones and animals and stuff . . .

He gets a shoebox and opens it. They both look inside expectantly.

KATHERINE: You invited me here to show me your . . . pet lizard?

HENRY: No, no, it's not mine. It's Johnny's. The guy across the hall. I just want you to see his tail.

KATHERINE: You stole Johnny's lizard / to show me its tail?

HENRY: No, Johnny's lizard *escaped*, and I found him in the kitchen, and I freaked out because I was chopping onions and he jumped—he fucking jumped—right onto the cutting board.

KATHERINE: They jump.

HENRY: Well, *I've* never had a lizard, so I didn't know that, and I freaked out and I chopped his tail off. *Right* off. And . . . it like kept wriggling. After I chopped it off.

KATHERINE: That's *autonomy*. Sacrifantes parte totum. (HENRY: Uh-huh.) Sacrificing a small part to protect the whole. (HENRY: Right.) The animal sheds or damages an appendage to protect itself. The hairy frog, for instance, breaks its own bones and shoves them through the skin to create claws.

HENRY: Well, that is fucking neat.

KATHERINE: *(finds it funny)* It is "neat."

HENRY: *(regretting his word choice)* Neat.

KATHERINE: Why didn't you give it back to Johnny?

HENRY: Um . . . "Hey, bud, here's half your lizard, sorry, hope that's okay?"—nope—but here's the thing, here's why I invited you—if you look here, you can see . . . he's . . .

KATHERINE: Growing it back?

HENRY: Yeah!

KATHERINE: They do that. Some of them, some species.

HENRY: That's normal? They just . . . grow another tail?

KATHERINE: Well, yes. But it's different—not quite as good as the other tail.

HENRY: Better than dying, I guess.

KATHERINE: It's not a sacrifice unless you lose something.

HENRY: I thought you'd be impressed. I thought I had discovered something new about lizards.

Beat.

KATHERINE: Did you. Did you really?

Beat. The jig is up.

HENRY: Hey, I thought that was good. I thought it was pretty good. *(beat)* Why would that be funny?

KATHERINE: What?

HENRY: Us sleeping together. Having sex.

KATHERINE: Is that why you invited me here?

HENRY: Course not. It was to see my groundbreaking discovery.

KATHERINE: The first of its kind.

HENRY: A zoological marvel.

KATHERINE: An osteological MIRACLE.

HENRY: Because I hold you in *such* high esteem.

KATHERINE: So you wouldn't feel taken advantage of if . . . ?

Beat. They laugh. This is a game of chicken.

HENRY: I can't stop thinking about you.

Beat.

KATHERINE: Is this a benchmark for you? Like a bucket list thing? Have sex with teacher—check. Have sex with woman over sixty—check check.

HENRY: *(incredulous)* You're over sixty?

KATHERINE: Oh, well done. Wash behind your ears.

HENRY: *(grinning)* Hey, we're animals. Beasts. Beasts with two backs, right? And we're attracted to each other.

KATHERINE: How do you know I'm attracted to you?

HENRY: I'm not an idiot.

KATHERINE: That's good, because I thought you stole a lizard and chopped off its tail to get me to sleep with you.

HENRY: I didn't steal it.

KATHERINE: How much was it?

HENRY: It was worth it.

Beat.

KATHERINE: You have no idea.

RAPP MEET CARSON

CARSON's office. RAPP has two coffees.

RAPP: You said cream and sugar, / right?

CARSON: Oh, no . . . just sweetener. / No milk.

RAPP: Aww fuck. I got you the / complete opposite.

CARSON: That's / okay . . .

RAPP: No, no, I can get you another one.

CARSON: It's okay, I'll drink it.

RAPP: Really?

CARSON: Sure, / thank you.

RAPP: Eh, better for you anyway, right? Aspartame gives you MS, all kinds of shit.

CARSON: Well, there's a history of diabetes in my family. So.

RAPP: And you wanna add MS? *(beat)* So, Detective Carson. You're in charge here?

CARSON: Yes. While my superior's on vacation.

RAPP: So, no you're not.

CARSON: Um . . . you're with the department in the city?

RAPP: No, no, I'm private, private investigator. Detective Rapp.

CARSON: Well no. (RAPP: Yeah.) No, you're not a *detective*.

RAPP: Well, yes, I am.

CARSON: But you're not a *police* detective.

RAPP: I didn't say I was a *police* detective.

CARSON: Do you correct people who assume you're / with the police—

RAPP: Look, you and me, we do the same thing except one of us has to play by the rules.

CARSON: I'm sorry, and you're here / to . . . ?

RAPP: To join forces. Put our heads together on the Kalles case.

CARSON: Oh, no, thank you. I've got it covered.

RAPP: You sure?

CARSON: Yup!

RAPP: Okay—

CARSON: Honestly, you seem a little young.

RAPP: Hey, you too, but I'm VERY good with missing persons. So good, in fact, that Mrs. Kalles of Kalles Yoghurt—you ever tried that yoghurt?

CARSON: No.

RAPP: Little sticks, like a freezie but it's yoghurt?*

CARSON: No.

RAPP: *UNREAL—anyway, I'm so good, *she* hired me to look into the disappearance of her son, Henry, who your department out here is having a hard time locating . . . hope that's not awkward.

Beat.

CARSON: Mr. Rapp—

RAPP: Detective.

CARSON: We . . . I have . . . reason to believe he is in Europe . . .

RAPP: Right, plane ticket to Prague the night of the fifteenth. Top *notch* police work, / you think . . .

CARSON: Ten thousand dollars cash withdrawn from / his bank account—

RAPP: Oh *my, ten thousand dollars*, sure looks like he was gonna stay / awhile.

CARSON: Okay, then his mother told you that he's done this before, yes? Twice, each time without notice—takes out cash so his mother can't track his cards.

RAPP: Sure, but she hasn't heard *anything* from him?

CARSON: We've called the embassy in Prague. Nothing.

RAPP: But we don't even know if he got on the plane. Because the day he left the airline's system got scrambled, right—which is crazy, and there's no passenger manifest for that flight the night of the fifteenth. (CARSON: Yes but—) The last time anyone saw him was that morning, here in Whittock.

CARSON: We've checked local hospitals and / ruled out—

RAPP: I mean he's the heir to the yoghurt empire—

CARSON: If he was kidnapped we'd have demands by now. Look, the kid went through a breakup—he just wanted to disappear somewhere.

RAPP: You don't think just *maybe* something happened to him? Mrs. Kalles's baby boy, her only son, who she loves more than life itself? (CARSON: Whom.) She's beside herself. She thinks he's dead, and it's been eleven days, so I'm inclined to think we're looking for a body.

CARSON: *We're* not looking for anything.

RAPP: You think he might have harmed himself?

CARSON: I doubt / it—

RAPP: Nah—this guy's got everything going for him—young, handsome, rich, smart. Valuable member of society. So I think it's gotta be good old-fashioned / mur—

CARSON: No, no, no. There's no motive. I spoke to his friends, his teachers . . . he's well-liked. Popular. Has no notable extracurriculars . . .

RAPP: His mother said he runs a podcast.

CARSON: I don't think of podcasting as a particularly treacherous business, do you?

RAPP: What about the ex? *(checks notes)* Pam Riley? She's here on a boxing scholarship? *(shadowboxing)* Hey, *she* could be dangerous.

CARSON: No. She doesn't like him, but I don't think she boxed him to death if / that's—

RAPP: So you think he could be dead?

CARSON: Anyone COULD be dead, but I don't think *he* is, and, honestly, Mr. Rapp, (RAPP: Detective.) I have other priorities at the moment.

RAPP: *Really?* In Whittock? You guys get a lot of action down here outside of the odd fender-bender? A couple drunk frat boys? *(clocking her gun)* You ever had to use that gun?

CARSON: You'd be / surprised.

RAPP: Because it feels like you're a little out your depth with a missing persons case. Your superior's out of town . . . it's a lot to handle . . .

CARSON: Well, I'm . . . handling it. I just think he's going to turn up somewhere, alive. That's my gut.

RAPP: Case closed?

CARSON: No, not . . . / case closed . . .

RAPP: Because then it was a *huge* waste of time making these.

He unfurls a large poster with HENRY's *face on it and pins it to something.*

CARSON: You cannot / put those up.

RAPP: Already did, all over town.

CARSON: There's a *procedure* / for—

RAPP: Oooh, sorry, a *procedure*—that must be a *police* thing.

CARSON: We have a social-media / alert—

RAPP: Yeah, but sometimes analogue really goes a long way in smaller communities, you know? Who knows, you may be right, he could be in Prague, but I'm just gonna speak to a few people . . .

CARSON: Which people?

RAPP: Well, it doesn't matter if we're not working together, right? Unless you're worried I'm gonna find out stuff you didn't and make you look worse than you already do, or we could do it *together*. I've worked with police tons—I'm very good at sharing. You might even like it!

CARSON: I won't.

RAPP: Two heads is better than one.

CARSON: I've got lots of . . . heads, thank you.

RAPP: You wanna try that again?

CARSON: No.

    CARSON pulls out an energy drink and chugs it.

RAPP: Okay, good chat. *(on his way out)* Jesus, energy drinks? Those'll kill you quicker than aspartame.

CARSON: We're dying the moment we're born! *(he's already gone)* Dammit.

PAM RILEY

The gym. PAM *is doing shadowboxing drills and sporadic push-ups. She is intense. The buzzer lets her know it's time to switch exercises.* RAPP *is watching her, comes over.*

RAPP: Pam? Pam Riley? (PAM: Yeah?) I just have a couple questions about Henry Kalles.

PAM: Why, *(punching)* did you find him? *(punch)* Is he dead?

Buzzer.

RAPP: That's kind of a shitty joke to make about someone who's missing.

PAM: Please, *(punch)* he's on a yoghurt-funded tour of Europe with some random girl!

RAPP: Why do you think that?

PAM: Because he wanted to take *me* once upon a time, okay?

RAPP: Miss Riley . . . May I call you Pam?

Buzzer.

Help me rule you out. I'm sorry, you're the only one with anything resembling a motive.

PAM: Because we *dated*? Come on, you think I disappeared him?

RAPP: Well, why'd you break up?

PAM: Hah. We *(punching)* drifted apart.

RAPP: I mean you clearly hate him.

PAM: Are you going to arrest every person that hates their ex?

RAPP: If their ex is missing, maybe.

    Buzzer.

PAM: Honestly, there are people in Whittock who hate Henry *(punching)* a hell of a lot more than I do.

RAPP: Oh yeah? You want to clarify that?

PAM: Didn't *(punching)* mean anything.

RAPP: Help me out here, Pam.

PAM: I can't.

RAPP: You're here on a scholarship, right? I can make this a lot harder for you.

    Buzzer. Beat.

PAM: I promised.

RAPP: Promised who? *(beat)* Okay, we can talk about it down at the station . . .

PAM: Are you fucking serious?

RAPP: What do you think?

    Beat.

PAM: You have to talk to the witch.

RAPP: The . . . witch?

PAM: The witch, yeah. And for the record, Henry and me dated casually, for like a second, and we were open, okay?

RAPP: Open?

PAM: Means you / can . . .

RAPP: No, I know what it means.

PAM: So, he was sleeping with *(punch)* lots of people.

RAPP: Like who?

PAM: Like everybody! Me, the girl down the hall. Move! He probably fucked the Boner Beast.

RAPP: The . . . Boner . . . ?

PAM: He interviewed her for his shitty podcast, and got, like, obsessed with her. She has sex with like five guys every year. It's fucking sad—like, get some self-respect.

Buzzer.

Those guys are just using you *(punch)* for a bar story.

RAPP: The Boner Beast is a . . . student?

PAM: You're the detective.

HEAD HAT

KATHERINE is giving a lecture to her class. She addresses us as if we are her students. She has a clicker. Maybe the sound of an old-timey slide projector changing slides.

KATHERINE: *(slide)* Nature teaches us that the best way to kill something is to be *invisible*, to disguise yourself as something that your prey simply *cannot* see. Am I boring you already, Joshua? No? Then put the phone away. Let's take the crab spider and their primary prey, the turtle ant. *(slide)* Now, the crab spider doesn't look very similar to the turtle ant— for starters, they have one less body segment. So, when the spider does manage to kill an ant, it doesn't eat it—not yet—it holds the ant corpse in such a manner that it appears, to the ant onlookers, as if their fellow ant's head is now the head of the spider. In short, it wears the ant as a hat. *(slide)* A hat. And it works.

RAPP sneaks in awkwardly. KATHERINE notices.

RAPP: Sorry! *(hushed)* Sorry.

He watches the remainder of the lecture from the house.

KATHERINE: Imagine if a human killer could do that. Wear the head of his kill to *blend* in. We, we don't know the difference—we just see a head, like any other head, and think to ourselves, no need to fear. Just another head, just another face, like mine—just another face—when underneath the crab spiders of the world, the invisible monsters, are biding their time, looking at all the little ants, knowing they're stronger, smarter, and more powerful, thinking to themselves . . . now this . . . *(beat)* this is going to hurt.

She changes slides with a click.

MEET KATHERINE

KATHERINE's office. RAPP holds two coffees.

RAPP: You said milk and sugar, / right?

KATHERINE: Oh, no . . . / black—

RAPP: Oh, fuck, sorry. I can go get you / another one.

KATHERINE: That's all right.

RAPP goes over and pokes at a fucking cool skeleton thingy.

RAPP: Your office is very fucking cool. This is a fucking cool . . . skeleton thingy . . . Was it like a / bird or . . .

KATHERINE: Please don't touch that.

RAPP: Sorry.

KATHERINE: You seem a little young to be a detective.

RAPP: *(takes a sip of coffee)* Blech! Oh, fuck me. Oh, this is *your* coffee! You must have mine. You wanna trade?

KATHERINE: No, / thank you.

RAPP: Come on, I just took one sip! What—you afraid I got cooties?

KATHERINE: I'm sorry, how old are you, Mr. Rapp?

RAPP: You can't just go around asking people how old they are—how old are YOU?

KATHERINE: Fifty-five.

RAPP: Well, you don't look a day over fifty.

KATHERINE: Well, thank you very much. I looked great at fifty.

RAPP: You look great now, and it's *Detective* Rapp . . . "How old are you, Detective Rapp." Like you didn't go through, what, a decade of training to be called *Mrs.* Yazov, right?

KATHERINE: *Ms.*, actually.

RAPP: Divorce?

KATHERINE: No.

RAPP: He died?

KATHERINE: No, there's no "he."

RAPP: *She* died?

KATHERINE: Someone has to die for me to be unmarried?

RAPP: "Yazov," that's . . . Russian?

KATHERINE: Originally, yes, but my family's Ukrainian.

RAPP: I love perogies.

KATHERINE: Yeah. Please call me Katherine. Everyone does, even my students.

RAPP: Got it, but I'm gonna call you *Dr. Katherine* then, you know, because we go through all this training to be official, right, to get, like, your doctor badge?

KATHERINE: We don't get badges.

RAPP: But wouldn't that be funny if a doctor had to, like, show you his badge—just a second, ma'am, let me just find my doctor badge—ah, shit! Where'd I put that fucking thing? *(as a nurse)* Doctor, doctor, he's bleeding out! Beeeepppp.

> *Beat.*

KATHERINE: I'm not that kind of doctor.

RAPP: Right, you're an *academic* doctor. You must be *very* smart.

KATHERINE: Oh, I am.

RAPP: What's your like . . . speciality?

KATHERINE: Osteology.

RAPP: Cancer.

KATHERINE: No, bones. And zoology is the other one—I believe you just observed a lecture of mine.

RAPP: Yeah, the "invisible monster." Cool stuff.

KATHERINE: Yes, it is.

RAPP: Hey, you saw me? I didn't just look like a student, on account of my youthful demeanour?

KATHERINE: I notice a new face.

RAPP: You must be very observant.

KATHERINE: Yes, I am. Sorry, am I being interrogated?

RAPP: No, no, I just have a few questions about a student. Are you single?

KATHERINE: That's relevant to your investigation?

RAPP: Yes, and I'm / just—

KATHERINE: I'm sorry, how old are you, Detective?

RAPP: Twenty-nine.

KATHERINE: Oh God, you're younger than my daughter.

RAPP: You have a *kid*!

KATHERINE: Yes, I'm *very* progressive, unmarried with a child. Can you just ask me questions like this?

RAPP: We're just chatting. Sparring. You don't like sparring with me?

KATHERINE: Oh, sure. You're affable enough.

RAPP: That's not a real word.

KATHERINE: Yes, it is.

RAPP: Sounds made up.

KATHERINE: No, it isn't.

RAPP: You're fucking with me.

KATHERINE: I wouldn't.

RAPP: Are you flirting with me?

Beat.

KATHERINE: No.

RAPP: Little bit?

KATHERINE: Detective, I don't like being teased.

RAPP: I'm not teasing.

RAPP: Did you want some harder questions?

KATHERINE: Sure.

RAPP: Some hard-hitting questions?

KATHERINE: All right.

RAPP: How old are you *really*?

KATHERINE: Sixty.

RAPP: You don't look a day over fifty-five.

KATHERINE: Thank you.

RAPP: What's your stance on abortion?

KATHERINE: Pro.

RAPP: Assisted suicide?

KATHERINE: Depends.

RAPP: Ethiopian.

KATHERINE: Food?

RAPP: Yes.

KATHERINE: Love it.

RAPP: Do you know any Henrys?

KATHERINE: . . . Yes.

RAPP: Henry Kalles?

KATHERINE: Well, I know he's missing—it's all over the school. Are you only just talking to people now?

RAPP: No, I'm only just talking to *you* now.

KATHERINE: Well, he's not *my* student—

RAPP: That's not what I asked—

KATHERINE: You think something happened to him?

RAPP: Like what?

KATHERINE: I . . . have no idea . . .

RAPP: We're investigating all avenues.

KATHERINE: Well, what can I do to help?

RAPP: How well would you say you know him?

KATHERINE: I / don't . . .

RAPP: *(listing)* Not well, well, like a brother, intimately, biblically?

KATHERINE: Not at all.

RAPP: Well, but . . . that's not really true. He interviewed you for his podcast a couple months ago—didn't he?

KATHERINE: Oh that. You listened to it?

RAPP: Yeah, but not *your* episode, because that's the weirdest thing . . . your name is there . . . the date . . . the subject . . . but you click on it, nothing happens. Dead link. How come?

KATHERINE: Technology, alas, is not my strong suit.

RAPP: Well, maybe you can fill me in on what you talked about.

KATHERINE: Bones.

RAPP: Well, not just bones, right? Baba Yaga. That's the name of the episode. I googled her. *(pulls out phone)* From Wikipedia: "In Slavic folklore, Baba Yaga is a supernatural being or one of a trio, appears as a deformed and ugly old woman, flies in a mortar, wields a *(pronounces it "pestal")* pestle"—

KATHERINE: Pestle.

RAPP: "Pestle," thank you. "Often seen in tales like 'Ivan the Bold.'"

KATHERINE: *(pronouncing it correctly: "Yvanne")* Ivan.

RAPP: *Ivan*, okay, so she's like a . . . ghost story?

KATHERINE: Or a fairy tale.

RAPP: Pretty fucked-up fairy tale . . .

KATHERINE: Most of them are.

RAPP: But she is a *witch*, right?

KATHERINE: People think so.

RAPP: Pam Riley said something about a witch.

KATHERINE: Pam Riley.

RAPP: Yeah, the boxer? She's the one who told me you were on the podcast.

KATHERINE: You're talking to me because I was on Henry's podcast? That's a crime?

RAPP: No, no. Although maybe it should be—that podcast is so bad it's *criminal*. But I was just speaking to some people and . . . I mean, you seem to have a bit of a . . . kind of a . . .

KATHERINE: A . . .

RAPP: Reputation.

KATHERINE: Do I?

RAPP: Don't they call you something? You know what it is, I don't need to / repeat—

KATHERINE: Lots of professors have / nicknames.

RAPP: Boner Beast?

KATHERINE: *Bone* Beast. Because I teach about *bones* and *animals*, and I'm tough. It's a joke.

RAPP: I don't get it.

KATHERINE: Who told you that? Pam Riley?

RAPP: Yeah, Henry's ex, you know her?

KATHERINE: Oh yes, Pam Riley *was* in my class. She hates me. (**RAPP:** Oh.) I failed her last semester. She has certifiable anger issues, and I've heard can be *quite* violent. (**RAPP:** Huh.) So, if I were you, I'd look into *her*.

RAPP: I'll keep my options open, but she also said that you and Henry maybe . . .

KATHERINE: You have an ambiguous nickname and a podcast interview and you're suggesting I . . . ?

RAPP: You're right, you're right, now that I've met you—seems unlikely, because you're *quite a bit* older—

KATHERINE: He's a student!

RAPP: Yeah, not your student—you're not some predator . . . I mean, technically you are in a position of authority, but because you're a woman it wouldn't be as creepy, even though he is, like, so much younger . . . What is he, twenty-one? Twenty-two?*

KATHERINE: I haven't a clue!

RAPP: *I'm saying if you *had* dipped a toe in . . .

KATHERINE: *(suddenly angry)* Now you listen, young man—*

RAPP: *Young man.* Wow . . .

KATHERINE: *—maybe you should check your sources before you go around making serious accusations that could affect / people's *livelihoods*—

RAPP: What exactly do you think I'm / accusing you of?

KATHERINE: I'm very sorry that boy is missing, and I sincerely hope you find him. If you'll excuse me, I have a class to teach.

RAPP: Take my card.

KATHERINE: I don't need it.

RAPP: Well, I'll just leave it here. In case you want to get Ethiopian sometime. *(on his way out)* Hey, you know about any witches here in Whittock?

KATHERINE: I'm sure I don't need to tell you this, Detective, but witches aren't real.

TRULY

Outside a duplex apartment. TRULY *has a plate with a Bundt cake.*

TRULY: *(mouth full)* The witch? Yer looking for Laney—'s what I call her—kids call her the witch. She's right upstairs, buzzer two.

RAPP: Oh, thank / you . . .

TRULY: But today she can't comma the door, on account of she ain't there. She's in the hospital, slipped in the tub, knocked her noggin, poor old thing, not that she's gonna knock looser anything that wa'nt loose already, mind ya. She's near on ninety-five—why? You think that was . . . foul play, do ya?*

RAPP: No . . .

TRULY: *Do ya?

RAPP: No.

TRULY: *Come on in! I'm Truly—yers truly! Want some Bundt cake?*

RAPP: No—

TRULY: *Foul play!

RAPP: No, no foul play. I'm just curious about her in relation to a missing student . . . Henry Kalles?

TRULY: Hmm, can't say I know a Henry. Knew a Hank, but it'd be a little late to be looking for him. He's been dead for years—hah! Siddown!

(handing him her Bundt cake) You have the rest of this piece. I'm not gonna finish it. (RAPP: No, that's—) Go on.

RAPP: *(tentative bite, mouth full)* Thank you. I'm just wondering what you can tell me about Laney aside from the spill.

TRULY: Why, you got a rash?

RAPP: A . . . rash? Me? No, no rash. Pamela Riley sent me. Do you know / her?

TRULY: Oh, she got a rash?

RAPP: There's no rash.

TRULY: Geez. Course, some of 'em come for other stuff. Headaches, arthritis. *(loud whisper)* GONORRHOEA.

RAPP: People come to her for . . . medicine?

TRULY: These days some people don't trust doctors and lotsa people come through—kids from the school—girls mostly. She's real good at helping women with womanly pains—meanin' PERIODS.

RAPP: Yes, / no, I understand.

TRULY: I been in there a coupla times myself, ya know. (RAPP: Yeah.) Sometimes I get pains in my koocheroo (RAPP: Yup.) like you wouldn't believe. (RAPP: Mm-hmm.) Meaning my *vagina*. (RAPP: Yeah.) And she gives me a *leaf* to chew—imagine that? A *leaf*. Whole place is fulla plants and flowers and such—she's a real nature path. Mind you, you do hear things. Like for the bigger stuff, she takes you . . . *outta* town.

RAPP: Outta town?

TRULY: Well, I don't wanna tell tales out of school. Now this was about five years ago, but I have a friend, Delia, she's good people, she runs a hardware store, and *her* friend Chelsea, who's put on a TON of weight, she said her hairdresser Annalise had a client, Shawna, who heard about a young gal who—

RAPP: What was *her* name?

TRULY: No idea, but Shawna says this young little gal gets knocked up by a POFS—meanin' piece of fucking shit. (RAPP: Right.) He fools around on her something awful and she do'en't want his baby but can't go to a doctor, so she comes in and ol' Laney tells her to come back at night, so she does, and Laney puts a *blindfold* on her and they get in a car and they drive forty-five minutes—end up at this little cabin in the mid-dl'a the woods—and there's—get this—*chickens* all over the damn place. Chickens—hah! *FOWL PLAY!* Hah! And Laney lights a fire in a big ol' pit, got all kinds of clay around it—

RAPP: Clay?

TRULY: —takes a burning stick and shoves it right down the chicken's throat, no word of a lie, and it's squawking something terrible. *(makes chicken squawking sound)* You could just hear it. (RAPP: Yeah.) *(squawk)* Then Laney takes a great big, you know, one of those things they use to whack through the jungle in movies?

RAPP: A ma/chete?

TRULY: A ma*shitty*, and she cuts open this squawkin' chicken's guts and pours 'em all over the gal's belly—then makes her drink something gets her all kinds of drunk. She passes out, next thing she knows, she wakes up as the car pulls back into town. And the next day, what do you think?

Beat.

RAPP: I honestly have no idea.

TRULY: Gal *miscarries*.

RAPP: How do you know she didn't just . . . lose it . . . naturally?

TRULY: S'pose we don't. But get this—a few weeks later . . . the POFs that knocked her up . . . guess what happened to him? *(beat)* Poof. Gone.

RAPP: He . . . died?

TRULY: No, stupid! Disappeared . . . All that's what Annalise said she *heard* anyway. Me? I'm just here. Minding my own business. And gossip is the devil's tool.

HELP

YAGA runs on stage screaming.

YAGA: *Help!*
My baby is dying.
Help.
My husband loves another.
Help.
My magical item is really hard to find.
Please.
Save my daughter.
Please.
Find my love.
Please.
Tell me the secret to make it all easier.
Give me.
The potions that prolong life.
Give me.
The swords to smite down mine enemy.
Give me.
The key to salvation.
They come.
In the night with desperate bargains and pleas.
They come.
With the promise of work or friendship or warmth.
They come.
And bristle at the slightest suggestion that they might have to work *just
a little* for what I have to give.

They take what they need
And they go.
Without so much as a fucking thank you.

Because let me tell you
No one wants to credit *a witch* with a happy ending.

And I wonder, I wonder why they tell stories about my cold, dark eyes, the ugly old virgin, the mother of monsters who eats their children as pay for their questions, when no one will stay and have a drink, get to know me.

I'm very funny, you know.

COP CHATS 1

Sandeson's Diner. RAPP *is at a table.* CARSON *comes in and sits down.*

CARSON: What?

RAPP: "Hi, thanks for calling, partner. Do you have some intel / about the—"

CARSON: We're not partners. I haven't had lunch.

RAPP: *(looking at menu)* I love places like this . . . classic diner meets old-timey dive bar. (**CARSON:** Uh-huh.) Kinda quaint and a little bit dirty . . .

Suddenly, GEENA *is there with menus.*

GEENA: Dirty?

CARSON: This is Geena. It's her place.

RAPP: *(recovering)* It's *so* great.

GEENA: Uh-huh. Welcome to Sandeson's. What'll you have?

CARSON: I'll have the burger, Geena.

GEENA: Okay.

CARSON: *(to* RAPP*)* Have the burger, get it bloody.

RAPP: Oh, no, thanks, I'm vegetarian. (**GEENA:** Oooh.) For ethical reasons.

GEENA: Oooh, ethics. Well, don't worry, buttercup, we kill 'em clean right out back. (RAPP: What?) Oh yeah, one good sledgehammer to the head—they go down like a ton of bricks.

Beat.

CARSON: She's kidding.

GEENA: I'm kidding.

RAPP: I'll have a water.

GEENA: One burger. Two waters. *(heading off)* Wasn't kiddin'.

Beat.

RAPP: Well, she's terrifying.

CARSON: Oh yeah. One time she stabbed a guy with a pair of tongs for getting too friendly with Lily.

RAPP: Lily?

CARSON: That's her daughter—she works here after school. She's a good kid.

RAPP: Geez, you know everybody?

CARSON: Grew up here.

RAPP: Wait, you're actually *from* / here?

CARSON: Anyway, she stabbed him right in the *eye*. With tongs.

RAPP: Huh. You got any?

CARSON: Tongs?

RAPP: Kids.

CARSON: *(ornery, he's prying)* Uh . . . No, do *you?*

RAPP: No. I'm just curious. You know, we're working together, kinda. Just trying to get to know you better.

CARSON: Why am I here, Rapp?

RAPP: Oh, I'm sorry. Here I thought I was being helpful, sharing my intel with you.

CARSON: Oh yeah, what do you got?

RAPP: Well, I guess I pressed Pam Riley a little harder than you did, because she said Henry was maybe fucking this older lady prof, Yazov, who he interviewed for his podcast about Baba Yaga—ugly old witch, kills people, grinds bones—but that episode is missing.

CARSON: Spooky.

RAPP: And this prof has an infinity for younger men—

CARSON: Affinity.

RAPP: Really?

CARSON: Yes.

RAPP: I've been saying that word wrong my entire life.

CARSON: Yeah, so you think the teacher was having an affair with Henry, the girlfriend got jealous, and . . . ?

RAPP: I dunno—Pam *hates* Henry, but it felt like she was covering for someone. She said there are other people who hate him more and that I should go to the witch.

GEENA comes back and drops their waters off.

GEENA: Why, you gotta rash?

RAPP: No I do not have a rash!

GEENA: Okay.

RAPP: *(to CARSON)* Does everybody know about the witch?

GEENA: She gave my Walter some kinda herb poultice once and he reeked like shit for a week. She give you a poultice?

RAPP: *No.*

GEENA: *(heading off)* Coulda fooled me.

RAPP: *(quiet, petulant)* I don't have a rash.

CARSON: Okay. The "witch" is a harmless old lady. My mom goes to her for migraines.

RAPP: Okay, well, her neighbour says she's in the hospital, so I call the hospital and they say, yeah, "Elena *Yazov* is here." Yazov. Same last name as the sexy professor—in a town this size? It's gotta be her mom or aunt or something . . . I'm going to go talk to the witch at the hospital, you wanna come?

CARSON: Oooh, you know I'd love to, but I have an interview with a vampire at the same time . . .

RAPP: Come on. Henry interviews Katherine Yazov about a witch, Pam Riley says a witch hates Henry, and there's a witch in town and she's related to Katherine Yazov? That doesn't have you a *little* curious?

CARSON: Geena, can you cancel that burger?

GEENA: *(yelling from off stage)* Please?

CARSON: Please! *(considers, then pulls out an envelope with RAPP's name written on it)* This came to the station for you.

RAPP: *(looks at her)* It's open.

CARSON: I had to make sure it was safe.

RAPP: *(pulling out a USB key)* Well, *thank you.*

CARSON: That's the podcast file that Henry and your sexy professor made.

RAPP: Wait, you *listened* to it?

CARSON: Yeah, while I was making the copy.

RAPP: Hey, someone sent that to ME!

CARSON: Well, I thought you wanted to co-operate with the police! Two heads, right? *(RAPP: Yeah, but you—) (gets up, pats him on the knee, heads off)* Good chat. Let's go see about a witch.

PODCAST

Sandeson's diner. KATHERINE *approaches* HENRY, *who's already at a table.*

KATHERINE: Henry?

HENRY: Hey! Dr. Yazov! I'm Henry! You already figured that out.

KATHERINE: *(shaking his hand)* Call me Katherine—is this place okay? Not too loud?

HENRY: Yeah, no, it's fine. This table is pretty quiet. Thank you so much for doing this.

KATHERINE: My pleasure.

HENRY: Okay, so the podcast is called *Lady Death Dealers in History: Fact or Fiction?* LDDIHFF, for short.*

KATHERINE: Okay . . .

HENRY: *Yeah, title needs work. So I'm a history major, and I'm really obsessed with, like, serial killers, (**KATHERINE:** Oh.) so each episode we take a different evil, murder-y mythological character and we figure out how they could actually have been inspired by real-life serial killers.

KATHERINE: So how can I help?

HENRY: Okay, do you mind if I start recording? (**KATHERINE:** No.)

He sets up a microphone/recorder on a mini tripod, hits record, and speaks more professionally.

I'm speaking with renowned osteologist Dr. Katherine Yazov.

KATHERINE: *(leaning in)* Hello.

HENRY: Oh . . . you don't have to lean in, it's a really good mic . . .

KATHERINE: Oh. / Sorry.

HENRY: So, first off, Katherine, let me ask you if you've ever heard of . . . *(pomp)* Baba Yaga.

KATHERINE: Yes.

HENRY: *(disappointed)* Really?

KATHERINE: *(matter of fact)* Yes—my mother is from Ukraine, so Yaga's in my bones, so to speak.

HENRY: Okay, so you know the etymology of "Baba Yaga," "Baba" meaning pretty universally "old woman" or "grandmother," and then "Yaga," which can mean all kinds of things—horror, shudder, chill, fury—

KATHERINE: Or it could be her name.

HENRY: Okay, like you'd be "Baba Katherine"?

KATHERINE: Oh, not yet. One day, hopefully.

LILY, fifteen, shy and awkward around HENRY, comes over holding a tray with two glasses of water. She has a dishrag in her back pocket. She looks at HENRY strangely.

LILY: Hi, I'm Lily. Welcome to Sandeson's. I'll be your . . . I'm gonna serve you . . . today . . . Do you need a few . . . / minutes?

HENRY: Hey, Lily, *(to KATHERINE)* whatever you'd like, my treat.

KATHERINE: Burger for me, please. Bloody.

HENRY: Me too. Same.

LILY: Okay . . . coming right up . . . Two blood burgers. Two bloody.

HENRY: Hey, it was . . . Lily? Sorry . . . these glasses are a bit dirty . . .

LILY: Oh . . . *(takes glass, spills it)* I'm . . . sorry.

HENRY: That's okay . . . It's totally fine. Oh, and this too, please. Just trying to spread out . . .

> *LILY looks at him, then goes off.*

KATHERINE: Wow. You really put her off her game.

HENRY: Me? How?

KATHERINE: Maybe she thinks you're cute.

HENRY: *(embarrassed)* No . . .

KATHERINE: Well, you know you are. (**HENRY:** No.) Handsome men always know they're handsome.

HENRY: Thank you. You too. Not handsome. I . . . Oh God. I mean, I . . . sorry. She's a little young for me anyway. (**KATHERINE:** Hm.) I like a *real* woman.

KATHERINE: *(smiling)* Oh?

HENRY: *(embarrassed)* I mean, oh. Um. Yeah.

> *Beat. HENRY clears his throat.*

HENRY: Yeah. Right. So Baba Yaga is a wicked, ugly old witch / who eats children . . .

KATHERINE: Well, it depends on which "witch"—ha!—story you're telling. Because she also helps people, when she wants to.

HENRY: Well in that "Ivan the Bold" story she's pretty evil.

KATHERINE: In that story, she wants to help *(pronouncing it correctly)* *Ivan* and sleep with him, and, yes, kill him, but ultimately she gives him the tools to escape—the *horns*, / which—

HENRY: Yeah, well, most people don't care about *that* Yaga, just the ugly, old, evil murder witch.

KATHERINE: *(sigh)* And *you* think she was a real-life serial killer?

HENRY: Yeah, okay, so my theory is: there's a record of a village in thirteenth-century Russia called . . . *(pulls out notepad)* oof, Kalach Nizhny—and around 1240 there's this old woman living in the woods outside of this village—and they called her . . . Babushka Urodlivaya— ugly grandma—and her house "kuryatnik"—chicken house.

KATHERINE: So she kept chickens, and was probably a wise woman. A healer.

HENRY: What?

KATHERINE: Well, if there's mention of her, the villagers might have gone to her to cure ailments / or other—

HENRY: Wait, why?

KATHERINE: Because history doesn't record women who live alone in the woods unless they do something for men.

HENRY: Yes. Yeah. Okay, so around the same time, there's reports of a bunch of people from that village just . . . disappearing. Going missing. Not dying of the plague, or whatever killed you in thirteenth-century Russia—

KATHERINE: I think everything killed you in thirteenth-century Russia.

HENRY: *(laughing)* Yeah, and, eventually, she finally died, and she was like *old*—we're talking *fifties*.

KATHERINE: Oh, that is old.

HENRY: Um. For thirteenth-century Russia? *Yeah*, so when she died, she just like . . . wandered into the middle of the village, lay down, and just . . . *expired*, and the townspeople went out to her hut in the woods, but it was just . . . poof.

KATHERINE: Poof.

HENRY: Gone. Like it was never there. *But*, underneath where it had been, scattered all around, they found—whoo boy—kurinyye per'ya—chicken feathers—and . . . kostnaya pyl—bone dust. *(spooky)* Oooohhh . . .

KATHERINE: So, you think this woman was your real-life Baba Yaga?

HENRY: I think she inspired it, anyway, and this, *this* is the reason you're really on the show, revered *osteologist* Katherine Yazov—what's goin' on with the *bones* . . .

KATHERINE: What do you mean?

HENRY: I . . . like what was she doing with them? How'd she grind them up?

KATHERINE: I hate to disappoint you, Henry, but *grinding* bones isn't really my / specialty.

HENRY: No, I know / but—

KATHERINE: You could talk to an engineer . . . or a nutritionist or . . .

HENRY: *(stops recording)* Come on, just try. Guess. Make up something *spooky!*

KATHERINE: Did you make all *that* up?

HENRY: No, no, of course not, not all of it, but you throw in some Google Russian in there and no one knows the difference.

He starts recording again, very serious.

So, Dr. Yazov, do you think she was *eating* the bones?

KATHERINE: *(struggling)* I . . . maybe . . . bones are chock full of nutrients. *(he mouths "spooky"; she tries)* She *could* have been eating—the marrow, or making—broth—and drinking it for . . . *(struggling)* digestion? . . . or . . . *power?* (HENRY: Power.) Consuming the *power* of those she killed . . .

HENRY: Good, and *how* do you think she ground them up?

KATHERINE: I haven't the slightest!

HENRY: Well, how would *you* do it?

KATHERINE: I . . . um . . . there's a piece of industrial agricultural equipment / called—

HENRY: *(stops recording)* Would they have had that in thirteenth-century Russia?

KATHERINE: Okay, okay. Okay. *(HENRY starts recording.)* My best guess is that she would . . . *(trying to be spooky) kill* (HENRY: Good.) the man. However she did that.

HENRY: Uh-huh.

KATHERINE: And then she'd . . . burn them first—the bones. She could burn the body . . . In a big fire. It would have to be *very* hot. Burning makes the bones brittle, easier to crack.

HENRY: Yes. Awesome.

KATHERINE: And then she would use a heavy object—

HENRY: Maybe the same object she used to kill the man?

KATHERINE: Sure . . .

HENRY: Like what?

KATHERINE: I . . . a rock *(He mouths "spooky" again.)* Or . . . a . . . *sledgehammer.* (**HENRY:** Sledgehammer?) And then she could . . . *(trying)* break up the bones until they were smaller—and then . . . she *could* have ground them in a mortar and pestle, if she wanted to. But goodness it would take forever . . .

HENRY: *(grinning, flirting)* Good, yes, but why spread them around your house?

KATHERINE: Uh . . . bone makes great fertilizer for gardening or . . . to avoid detection, I suppose—harder to find bone dust than bodies . . . *(spooky, sexy, looking at him)* or maybe . . . she just liked how it felt between her *toes.*

HENRY turns off the recorder.

Was that all right?

HENRY: That was *perfect.* You sounded great, really, thank you for being such a good sport.

He starts to pack up his equipment.

KATHERINE: What on earth made you think of Baba Yaga?

HENRY: Oh! She's a villain in video games and in *John Wick* and in *Arthur*. She just kinda popped into my head one day, (KATHERINE: Hm.) it was super random. But turns out the actual Baba Yaga is, like, very, very cool.

KATHERINE: Because you think she's a *serial* killer?

HENRY: Yeah, because serial killers are cool and people want to know stuff about them, like what makes them tick.

KATHERINE: But *you* don't care about what makes her tick.

HENRY: No, I do, it's just more fun if she's just evil!

KATHERINE: You don't wonder . . . why?

HENRY: She doesn't *need* / a reason.

KATHERINE: Boredom? Fun? Revenge? Did she have family? Children?

HENRY: What? No! She wasn't a *mom*. She was a wicked old witch in the woods!

KATHERINE: She isn't *always* wicked . . .

HENRY: It's more fun if she is.

KATHERINE: Is it?

HENRY: *(laughing, awkward)* I thought bad girls had more fun.

KATHERINE: *(flirting back)* Yes. We usually do.

HENRY: I'm gonna check on our waters . . . *(beat) Hey,* if you have some time in the next week or so . . . can I show you something?

HE SAID

YAGA: It was night when he came, running, bloody, hungry
I said he could rest
I said I would hide him
I said I would help
He had a black cloak with red inside
He ate my vegetables
But they weren't enough, he said
He wanted meat, he said
So he killed a chicken
He didn't ask—he killed a chicken
He ate the chicken and then he was tired so he slept by the fire
But it wasn't warm enough, he said
So he came to my bed
To be near, he said
For warmth, he said
It's not enough, he said
He wanted warmth
He wanted meat
And he was strong

He didn't ask to kill the chicken

But later
When he slept
I showed him I could be strong too

He had a black cloak with red inside
And he was gone

But I wasn't alone anymore.

ELENA 1

Hospital.

RAPP: Listen, why don't you let me run point on this one, okay?

CARSON: I know her.

RAPP: Yeah, but it's my lead—I talked to Truly.

CARSON: Okay, it's your lead.

RAPP: Thank you very much.

ELENA enters with a rolling IV unit, or starts to stir in a hospital bed. She speaks with a thick Ukrainian accent. (Translations in square brackets.)

CARSON: Elena! Let me help you . . .

RAPP: Elena Yazov? Mrs. Yazov.

ELENA: *(spits)* Nemaye muzha. No husband. *Ms.*

RAPP: Sorry, *Ms.* Yazov. I'm Detective Rapp—

ELENA: *(looking at him)* I know *you*. I know who *you* are. *(to CARSON, gesturing to RAPP)* Harne. *[Handsome.]*

CARSON: Oh, no, we're not *together.*

RAPP: We're just partners.

CARSON: No, we're *not*, don't confuse her. (**RAPP:** It's a new thing) Hello, *Ms*. Yazov, I'm Detective Carson.

ELENA: *(to CARSON)* Clever?

CARSON: He's all right.

ELENA: *(to CARSON)* Day menu spaty. *[Let me sleep.]*

RAPP takes out his phone and starts recording.

CARSON: Rapp, you can't / record this!

RAPP: We have no idea what she's saying!

ELENA: Soon, it will be too late. *(to RAPP)* She knows this, still she waits.

RAPP: Who's / she?

CARSON: We're just here to ask you a few questions. Is that all right?

ELENA: You bring podarunok? *(CARSON and RAPP look at each other blankly.)* When you ask for something you should bring *gift*, for thank you. You bring *gift*?

RAPP: I'm sorry, we didn't / think—

ELENA: No, my'aso? No kvity? No vodka? Nobody brings me vodka. As usual. Okay. Ask questions. *(to CARSON)* Always he has questions.

RAPP: Katherine Yazov is your daughter?

ELENA: Tak. Katya. Dotsia. *[Daughter.]*

RAPP: And you're originally from Ukraine . . . is that right?

ELENA: Tak. I come z mamoyu. With Mama. No Bat'ko. No Papa.

CARSON: Ms. Yazov, we're investigating the disappearance of Henry Kalles...

ELENA: *(spit)* Bad dog.

RAPP: You know him?

ELENA: *(secretive, with relish)* She take his teeth out with hammer.

RAPP: The ... bad dog's ... teeth?

CARSON: Who did?

ELENA: Naymolodsha onutsia. *[Youngest granddaughter.]* So he could not bite anyone else. *(She suddenly bites at the air like a dog.)* Now I am tired. I cannot do *my* work. Only waiting for Ivan.

RAPP: Who is Ivan? The bad dog?

CARSON: We're looking for Henry / ... not Ivan.

ELENA: *(to RAPP)* I think she like you?

CARSON: No, no, I don't.

ELENA: *(to CARSON)* Handsome. Strong. *(manhandling him a bit)* But he never asks the right question.

RAPP: *(laughing)* Uh ... I'm ... trying. Pam Riley—do you know her? The boxer? *(ELENA spits.)* Right. Well, she thinks maybe *you* didn't like Henry.

ELENA: No one like bad dog. Handsome. Clever. Good for the chickens.

RAPP: Your neighbour ... Truly, she says you help people. Women. With ... problems. In the woods. With their babies ...?

CARSON: *(whispering quickly)* You sound insane.

RAPP: *(whispering)* Shut up.

ELENA: Kvitka never saying thank you. They never say. *(to RAPP)* Take me to window.

> *RAPP goes over as ELENA struggles out of bed.*

RAPP: She wants to!

CARSON: Just be careful!

ELENA: Oooh, feel his strong arms . . . *(to RAPP)* I was young too, you know. Beautiful. Still she waits—she is angry. But we are all angry when we are young. Kvitka is young—she didn't want it. Take baby, kill dog, they never say thank you! *(spits)* What do I care? I wait for Ivan.

RAPP: Ivan . . . Ivan? Like Ivan the Bold?

ELENA: *(correcting him)* Ivan.

RAPP: From Baba Yaga?

ELENA: Baba *Yaha*.

CARSON: Ughh. Rapp, leave it alone.

RAPP: Can you tell me about Baba Yaga?

CARSON: *(annoyed)* Oh my God.

ELENA: My vsy yaha. *[We are all yaga.]* I am babusia, lehenda. But I should not be so old. Is time for dytia *[baby]*. I want to sleep.

CARSON: You heard her, she wants to sleep . . .

RAPP: Just . . . Did your daughter have a . . . relationship with Henry Kalles?

ELENA: *(giggles)* She like when they are young and handsome. I like too!

RAPP: Did Katherine kill the bad dog?

ELENA: No, stupid! Is not her job. You end with the hammer, as usual!

CARSON: Okay, we're upsetting her.

RAPP: We don't mean to make you angry—

ELENA: Ne serdyt'sia! *[Not angry!]* She is the angry one. Molodsha. But now she must make dytia. Zavzhdy maye buty troya. *[She must always be three.]* She knows this.

RAPP: Who is *she*? Katherine?

CARSON: Rapp / stop—

ELENA is getting really worked up.

ELENA: *(to CARSON)* U vas ne vystachaye chasu. *[You are running out of time.]*

CARSON: I'm going to get someone.

ELENA: *(to RAPP, quickly)* You are good dog. Come back, bring podarunok—kvity, my'aso, vodka. Ask me the *right* question, don't look for bad dog—he is dust in the woods for the chickens.

RAPP: But who killed the bad dog?

ELENA: *(a beat, smiles and whispers)* Baba Yaha. *(moves away, unsteadily)* She take too long, but still I love her. Family is family. What can you do?

JANICE / COP CHATS 2

CARSON's office.

RAPP: Carson.

CARSON: Rapp.

RAPP: Carson.

CARSON: Do you have any idea how much trouble I'm in?*

RAPP: Carson.

CARSON: *Apparently we sent Elena into some kind of "episode." (**RAPP:** Carson) The hospital had to call Katherine / Yazov—

RAPP: CARSON.

CARSON: What?

RAPP: There's someone I want you to meet.

CARSON: Who?

JANICE: *(coming in)* Hullo.

Beat.

RAPP: This here is Janice. Janice, this is *Police Detective* Carson.

CARSON: Hi, Janice.

JANICE: Hullo.

RAPP: Have a seat, Janice. Janice drives a truck, don'tcha, Janice.

JANICE: Yeah.

RAPP: Tell her what kinda truck, Janice?

JANICE: Oh, a loggin' truck with an integrated flatbed—

RAPP: And what route do you take, Janice?

JANICE: Yeah, straight up the 701 up through the woods up by there.

RAPP: And, Janice, can you tell me what you saw on the 701 when you were up through the woods up by there?

JANICE: Uh, which time?

RAPP: The . . . the time we talked about, Janice, the time we *just* talked / about.

JANICE: Oh . . . yeah, yeah, so, I was coming around a bend, right where the 701 crosses the road that takes you up to the cliffs up by there, and, yeah, I thought I saw . . . you know a . . . guy.

RAPP: *(proudly, to CARSON)* A GUY!

CARSON: A guy.

JANICE: Yeah.

RAPP: And what did this guy look like, Janice?

JANICE: Oh, uh . . . young. Brown hair. Good looking. Real nice body.

RAPP: Well, how'd you know he had a real nice body, Janice?

JANICE: *(blushing furiously)* Oh . . . yeah, cuz he was . . . naked.

RAPP: NAKED! Now why on earth wouldn't you stop to help him if he was naked, Janice?

JANICE: Oh, yeah, I . . . well, I'm not really in the habit of picking up naked men in my truck. (**RAPP:** Course not.) He wasn't, well . . . he didn't look like he was in *trouble*.

RAPP: Naked in the woods in the middle of the night, all alone?

JANICE: Well, he wasn't *alone*.

RAPP: No?

JANICE: He was with someone.

RAPP: Who?

JANICE: A lady, I thought.

RAPP: A LADY!

CARSON: A lady?

JANICE: Yeah, looked like they were playin' a game or something. He looked like he was out of it . . . I thought maybe he was on the drugs, and that's okay, you know, sometimes I like to take a puff of / something—

CARSON: Okay, what did the lady look like?

JANICE: Didn't get a good look at her . . . He was slow, she was quick.

CARSON: Well, how'd you know it was a lady then.

JANICE: Well, the hips.

CARSON: The hips.

CARSON *downs another energy drink.*

RAPP: And when was this, Janice?

JANICE: In the middl'a . . . the . . . night.

RAPP: No, no, what *date*, Janice.

JANICE: Oh, the fifteenth.

RAPP: Nope.

JANICE: Oh, the middl'a of the night. So . . . sixteenth.

RAPP: Yes! Middle of the night on the *sixteenth*, right. Now, Janice, can you tell me when you saw that guy again?

JANICE: Oh I didn't see him again.

RAPP: Yes you did.

JANICE: Oh, you mean just his face.

RAPP: Yeah, just his face.

JANICE: Oh, on the poster!

RAPP: On the POSTER! And is *this* the guy you saw? *(triumphantly points to the poster he pinned up earlier)* On the *sixteenth* of this month, where the 701 meets the road that takes you up to the cliffs up by there?

JANICE: Yeah.

RAPP: Right. Right. Thank you very much, Janice, you've been *very* helpful. Thank you so much for calling me and coming in today. You are a very good person and a wonderful concerned citizen, and I hope you have a fabulous life.

JANICE: Yeah, that's all good, the uh . . . reward . . . ?

RAPP: *(ushering her out)* We'll send you an e-transfer.

JANICE: Oh . . . You got my email?

RAPP: Yeah.

JANICE: Okay.

She goes.

RAPP: Eh?

CARSON: Are you very proud of yourself?

RAPP: Are you kidding? She saw Henry out in the woods on the sixteenth, so he definitely wasn't on a plane to Prague on the fifteenth, was he? Elena said "the dog was dust for the chickens in the woods"! So do you think maybe we should check the woods out by the 701 up by there?

CARSON: For *dust*?

RAPP: For a *body*!

CARSON: Yeah, we'll check the woods.

RAPP: Great idea. I'll bet you anything that lady she saw was Katherine Yazov. Or . . . it *could* even be Elena Yazov . . .

CARSON: Elena is a million years old. She's not quick. I doubt she was canoodling in the woods—

RAPP: Canoodling.

CARSON: Yes, canoodling.

RAPP: But we don't know they were "canoodling." Maybe . . . Henry goes to Elena with a rash . . . Truly said some guy disappeared from Whittock five years ago, after his girl went to Elena . . .

CARSON: She could mean David Becker. (RAPP: Who?) He went missing around five years ago. I had just started with the department.

RAPP: Maybe you could look into that case file for me . . . partner?

CARSON: Okay, I'll see what I can do.

RAPP: Okay, stay with me. Elena said Henry's a bad dog. What does that mean?

CARSON: Maybe she knew he was sleeping with her daughter—maybe Henry was threatening to tell the administration . . .

RAPP: So maybe Elena kills him to protect Katherine. But she says Baba Yaga killed the dog. So who is Baba Yaga? (CARSON: What?) And who is Ivan?

CARSON: Rapp, Elena is not mentally sound, and neither are you if you think this is about Baba Yaga!

RAPP: Someone sent me that podcast for a reason . . .

CARSON: So, should we look for a magical chicken house?

RAPP: Nah, we don't know the magic words . . . *(flirty)* But we *could* just wander through the woods trying stuff out—what are you doing later? *(CARSON laughs.)* I know it sounds crazy, but I bet there's something *here*. Elena's "witch," there's a cabin in the woods, Katherine teaches *bones*. She's got this like . . . witchy energy . . .

CARSON: *Energy?*

RAPP: I've been Google-translating Elena's recording—there must always be three, she said. It's not *Katherine's* job to kill the dog, Elena said, so whose job is it? She's talking about it like there's another person.

CARSON: Now there's a contract killer?

RAPP: *(gets a text)* Speak of the devil. Katherine Yazov.

CARSON: I'm sorry, is she *texting* you?

RAPP: I gave her my card. She . . . *(reading)* wants me to come for dinner.

CARSON: Well, you can't go!

RAPP: I have to talk to her again anyway.

CARSON: Yeah, I bet you do. *(off his look)* Sure, go. She does have an *infinity* for young men . . . Just remember the last guy she went out with ended up missing.

RAPP: I think I can handle her.

CARSON: Maybe that's just what she wants you to *(He's already gone.)* think. Dammit.

INVISIBLE

KATHERINE's house. She's cooking, chopping something with a large kitchen knife. Music. RAPP brought a bottle of wine.

KATHERINE: I hope you don't mind coming here. There's a shortage of Ethiopian restaurants in Whittock. But it's vegetarian. (**RAPP:** How did . . .) *(off his look)* Small town. Oh, thanks. You can go ahead and open that. Let it breathe.

RAPP: I'm surprised you called.

KATHERINE: Well, you didn't have to come.

RAPP: It's not every day you get invited to dinner by a suspect, so it's police procedure to say yes.

KATHERINE: I'm a suspect now?

RAPP: Well, I'm investigating the disappearance of your *boyfriend* so . . .

KATHERINE: He isn't my boyfriend.

RAPP: Alleged fuck buddy, then.

KATHERINE: What would you think if I had fucked him?

Beat.

RAPP: I guess I'd think I had a shot.

KATHERINE: Did you think this was a *date*, Detective?

RAPP: Isn't it?

KATHERINE: I didn't know that was on offer. I just wanted to talk.

RAPP: Oh, me too. *(She pulls out a mortar and pestle.)* Hey, you got a mortar and *(pronounces it "pestal" again)* pestle.

KATHERINE: Pestle.

RAPP: Pestle. Right.

KATHERINE: I'll make sure to sweep all the bones out first . . .

KATHERINE & RAPP: *(cheersing their wine glasses)* Cheers.

RAPP: Hah, hey, could you tell me where you were on the night of the fifteenth, morning of the sixteenth real quick? Just so that's out of the way.

KATHERINE: *(thinks)* I was at a friend's cottage. Professor Murray. We had a lot of wine, I stayed over.

RAPP: Did he make a move?

KATHERINE: He's a friend and he's *eighty*—

RAPP: Don't be ageist.

KATHERINE: —and *gay*, and you can go ahead and corroborate that with him.

RAPP: That'd be a weird conversation . . .

KATHERINE: I hear you went to see my mother.

RAPP: Ah, no, see, I went to see the Witch of Whittock—I didn't know she was your mother. I asked you about the Witch—

KATHERINE: You asked me if I *knew* of any witches in Whittock, and since I don't put stock in cruel nicknames, I didn't know you meant my mother . . .

RAPP: Sure, but why wouldn't you mention she lives here?

KATHERINE: Because you didn't ask? Parents should be close to their children. She goes where I go.

RAPP: Everywhere?

KATHERINE: Of course not *everywhere*, but when I go to a new school, she comes, yes.

RAPP: New school—isn't the whole point to get . . . tender?

KATHERINE: Tenure? (RAPP: Yeah.) I don't like being tied down—listen, my mother is not well, and you had no / right—

RAPP: I know, I'm sorry—nasty spill in the tub—she was okay to answer our questions . . . We found her downright chatty, in fact.

KATHERINE: We?

RAPP: Oh, I'm working with a local detective out here, Carson.

KATHERINE: Oh. Is she pretty?

RAPP: How'd you know she was a she?

KATHERINE: Just how you said her name. I'm very observant, remember?

RAPP: Yeah. She's kind of pretty. Very tough. A bit . . . tight. (KATHERINE: Tight.) Anyway, your mum was very disappointed we didn't bring . . . kvitky? Flowers, right? I Google-translated it. It was *really* hard.

KATHERINE: Good for you.

RAPP: *And* she thinks I'm handsome.

KATHERINE: Well, she has dementia.

RAPP: *(offended)* Well she seemed pretty lucid to me. I'm sure you know she's been curing rashes in Whittock?

KATHERINE: Do you have / a rash?

RAPP: No. No. NO. I do not have a rash, (KATHERINE: Oh.) and she's also performing strange rituals involving killing chickens to get / rid of—

KATHERINE: Listen—

RAPP: What about David Becker? Know anything about him?

KATHERINE: I don't know who that is. Detective, there will always be rumours, in any small town, especially about women who live on their own and do what they want. My mother is a very gifted naturopath. It makes her happy. She's had a hard life, and she's dying, Detective. Please stay away from her.

RAPP: *She's* got a lot to say about Baba Yaga. So did you. On the podcast.

KATHERINE: I thought that episode was missing.

RAPP: Someone sent it to me anonymously. It's fascinating. Kind of flirty. Henry sounds like an idiot, but you seem to know a lot about her.

KATHERINE: Millions of people all over the world know about her.

RAPP: Yeah, it's just . . . It almost felt like you were defending her.

KATHERINE: Well, I like her. She resonates with me. With most women, I think. A female figure of great power. Wisdom. Rage.

RAPP: What, are you angry about something?

KATHERINE: Women? Oh, we're angry about everything. *(beat)* You're looking for Henry, and my mother doesn't know him.

RAPP: Really? Because she seems to think you did have a relationship and that Baba Yaga killed him, and he's dust in the woods.

KATHERINE: My mother buried the TV remote in the park and stood over it telling it to fly.

RAPP: Okay, so who's Ivan? She said she's waiting for Ivan.

KATHERINE: It's another Yaga story. Ivan the Bold. Shall I tell it to you? A bedtime story, little boy?

RAPP: I hope so. You know, I'm really enjoying getting to know her. Baba Yaga.

Beat.

KATHERINE: And what do *you* think of her?

RAPP: I agree with what you said—she's a bit misunderstood. Like your mother. Like you.

KATHERINE: Surely you're not suggesting that my mother is a real-life Baba Yaga. Or that I am? Do you think I'm a witch, Detective?

RAPP: No, / I'm saying—

KATHERINE: What happens next? Villagers organize a witch hunt and burn me at the stake for daring to enjoy life—a career, family, and *(gasp)* good sex after menopause?

RAPP: No, / okay.

KATHERINE: I must be a witch. That's the only way that a handsome twenty-two-year-old *might* have fucked me? Did he fuck my mother too?

RAPP: Okay, okay, but you wouldn't happen to *have* a magic cabin in the woods, wouldja?

KATHERINE: If I did, you'd need the magic words, and If I told you those I'd have to kill you.

RAPP: How about a couple of witchy sisters? Elena kept saying "molodsha"—that's "youngest," right? Any chance you have an angry younger sister who kills dogs with hammers?

KATHERINE: Hate to disappoint you—only child, or couldn't you tell?

RAPP: Hah. *(cheerful)* But what about your daughter? *(beat)* That's not a secret, right? When you first met me, you said I was younger than your daughter, and then your mother said "onutsia."

KATHERINE: I suppose you googled it.

RAPP: Granddaughter. And Elena is babusia, grandmother. She says "onutsia" took the dog's teeth out with a hammer. That she's the angry one.

KATHERINE: Look, my mother and Anna . . . they don't get along. It's a generational thing.

RAPP: Anna.

KATHERINE: Yes, that's her name. She lives in Europe.

RAPP: Any chance she happens to know Henry?

KATHERINE: She met him once, on a recent visit.

RAPP: How'd she feel about him?

KATHERINE: I don't know, you'd have to ask her.

RAPP: I will.

KATHERINE: Good, please let me know when you reach her. She's not answering my calls. I think she's mad at me about something.

RAPP: Aren't you worried about her?

KATHERINE: Oh, no, she's very capable.

RAPP: Well, when was the last time you spoke?

KATHERINE: *(thinks)* Maybe a month ago. *(fake gasp)* I suppose around after she met Henry.

   Beat.

RAPP: I . . . Katherine, come on! Why wouldn't you mention that your daughter knew Henry?

KATHERINE: Why? Is she a witch too?

RAPP: I just . . . is this fun for you?

KATHERINE: Which, the date or the investigation?

RAPP: This would be a lot easier if you'd just tell me everything you know so that things don't look worse for you and your family.

KATHERINE: Now you want to *help* my family.

RAPP: No, I want to help *you*.

KATHERINE: Why?

RAPP: I don't know. I guess I feel sorry for you.

KATHERINE: Well, don't.

RAPP: No. You're clearly brilliant, you're stuck out in this town in butt-fuck nowhere, looking after your mother, sleeping with students—what, because you're bored? Isn't that why you're here with me?

KATHERINE: What if I think you're interesting? What if I like "sparring" with someone clever? And handsome?

RAPP: No. I think you talk a big game, but you're scared.

KATHERINE: I'm not scared of anything. And it's not boredom. It's nice to be seen.

RAPP: Seen.

KATHERINE: You know, there's a time in a woman's life when people just stop . . . seeing you. Completely. You're no longer the maiden—not a sexual object—you're not the mother—no longer fertile—so no longer useful . . . then . . . what are you? The crone. Invisible. Henry *saw* me.

> Beat. RAPP *laughs.*

RAPP: Henry "saw" you? Come on. Fuck that. You are the most interesting person I've met in a long time. You couldn't be invisible if you tried.

KATHERINE: Because I have cool skeletons in my office?

RAPP: Because you're beautiful, and smart, and I can see your mind working furiously every time I look at you.

KATHERINE: That's a very good compliment.

RAPP: Yeah, it is.

KATHERINE: You don't beat around the bush.

RAPP: I don't see why I should. What, you don't like me? I'm very likeable. Someone once told me I was *affable*.

He comes close to her.

KATHERINE: What are you doing, Detective?

RAPP: I . . . don't know. Seeing you.

He comes toward her.

KATHERINE: Is *this* police proc—

He kisses her. It's a really great kiss.

Well. If you thought my office was cool . . . you should see my bedroom.

Intermission.

ACT TWO

CHILDLESS WITCHES

YAGA comes across the stage. We're still in house lights. She speaks directly to us, getting us to sit down, etc. She pours and takes a few shots of Ukrainian vodka over the course of this monologue.

YAGA: Hey! Hey! Hey! Let me ask you. *(light shift)* Do you have child? Or are you childless?

What a thing to say. As if you're somehow *less* without child.

But, let's talk about childless *witches*.

Childless witch helps two kids escape their shitty parents, lets them eat her nice candy house, she gets burnt to a crisp.

Childless witch helps royal couple get child, doesn't get an invite to the christening, organizes a nice long nap for princess, witch gets sword-skewered by a prince.

Childless witch *protects* young girl by putting her in a nice tower, girl gets knocked up by prince, witch loses her forever.

Things do not work out well for childless witches.

But can you think of any other kind?

When was the last time you heard of a wicked witch . . . with a baby? A *mother* witch? I mean honest-to-God practises-magic-dances-with-the-devil witch . . . who is also a card-carrying member of *reproductive* society? *Never*.

So, we get pushed into ovens, stabbed with swords, and chased by dwarves—little fuckers.

So, why not just have kids? Why not pop out a few buns, if only to delay the stake, the cross, the rack.

WHY NOT?

Is it a biological issue? Are we all somehow, truly barren? When you make that deal with the devil does she take your *uterus*?

She takes a shot.

No! Of course not.
Or is it that no one will fuck us? Because we are evil, or have bad manners and don't floss?

She takes a shot.

No! Of course not!
Is it because we are old, and ugly, as the stories KEEP REMINDING US?
Because we have teeth where our pussies should be?
No! Of course not!
We have magic, motherfuckers—we are fascinating and sing beautifully.
We talk to the trees and have MANY EXOTIC PETS.
Then is it . . . that the men who tell our stories are . . . *scared* of us?
And a witch with a child . . . that would really scare them . . .
Because they know that through children we will live forever.
And they'd rather we . . .
Poof.
Disappear.
Better to say we *eat* children than that we *have* children.
So it seems to me, to *us*, that the first thing you should concern yourself with, as a witch—

She raises the final shot to us.

Is how to live forever.

PRETTY WOMAN

We're in a fancy restaurant. Classical music plays. ANNA's *at the bar. She has a bottle of wine and two glasses.* HENRY, *at a table, tries to get the waiter's attention, is snubbed, gives up.*

ANNA: Um. It's because he thinks you're being stood-up. That's why you can't get the waiter's attention.

HENRY: I'm not . . . / being stood up.

ANNA: Okay. Do you want some wine while you wait? I got a whole bottle, you can just have some. I won't like, sit with you. I'm meeting my mom . . . *(pours, stands awkwardly)* (HENRY: Thank you.) Who are *you* waiting for?

HENRY: My . . . uh . . . I guess she's my girlfriend / sort of—

ANNA: Oh. Sorry, that's awkward, you have a girlfriend.

HENRY: It's okay. I'm actually meeting . . . her kid.

ANNA: Oh, she's got a little kid.

HENRY: *(looking at her)* The kid's not . . . little. (ANNA: Okay.) You said you're meeting your . . . mother?

Beat. At some point ANNA *comes over and sits at* HENRY's *table.*

ANNA: Oh. Come on. No. Ughh. FUCK OFF, MOM. OHMYGOD. (HENRY: What?) She knew if she *told* me I wouldn't come and now she's fucking late on purpose!

HENRY: No, no, I'm . . . *early!*

ANNA: You're an idiot if you think you were even half a step ahead of her.

HENRY: No. I'm . . . smart . . . It was my / idea . . .

ANNA: Yeah, she wants you to *think* it's your idea. Ughh. What a DICK.

HENRY: I'm not!

ANNA: No, *her*. *(pours herself a glass of wine, chugs)* This is *such* a dick move.

HENRY: Well, anyway, I'm Henry, it's nice to / meet you . . .

ANNA: What are you, like, eighteen?

HENRY: I'm twenty-two!

ANNA: *Mother!*

HENRY: What? We're two of-age people—

ANNA: Having an affair.

HENRY: No, we're not *cheating* / on other people.

ANNA: An affair is a romantic or passionate entanglement typically of *limited* duration.

HENRY: What are you, a dictionary?

ANNA: OMG, you *are* smart. How can my genius mother possibly hope to keep up with someone whose best insult is calling someone a DICTIONARY?

HENRY: Okay, it's not my *best insult*, and I don't need your permission.

ANNA: Well, good, you don't have it.

HENRY: Well . . . what are you gonna do?

ANNA: I dunno, maybe I'll tell someone about it.

HENRY: It's not against the law. I'm not her student.

ANNA: But you are *a* student, right? She could still be fired. So.

HENRY: You'd do that?

ANNA: Ugh. No. She can have her fun—she always does. You know she's done this before, right?

HENRY: Yeah. I know that.

ANNA: Loads of times. Every school she's ever been at. (**HENRY:** Okay.) She will honestly sleep with anyone.*

HENRY: Okay, that's—

ANNA: *So I can keep a secret if you can. The royal you, *all* the men, so many men. (**HENRY:** I . . .) More wine?

HENRY: No, I'm not finished my / first—

ANNA: *(pouring)* So you have a thing for older women?

HENRY: I have a thing for your mom . . . I mean she's incredible.

ANNA: You don't think she's scary?

HENRY: No.

ANNA: I've seen her crack open a human breastbone with a hammer— that's scary. Like, the human was dead. Before, I mean. And after too. Still.

HENRY: That's good. Not a necromancer, that's good.

They laugh. The mood lightens.

I'm sorry, I'm just trying to imagine your mother hacking open a chest with a hammer. I mean *you* . . . you look strong. I mean, that's . . . a compliment. What is that, Pilates?

ANNA: Boxing. (HENRY: Oh.) But my *mom's* very good with a hammer and a master of manipulation.

HENRY: If you guys don't get along, why would you meet her for dinner?

ANNA: Family's family. You love to hate 'em, but they're yours forever, you know?

HENRY: But this whole thing bothers you.

ANNA: Wouldn't it bother you if your mother was fucking people younger than *you*? (HENRY: I . . .) And it *should* bother you—think about it, when you're in your prime she'll be in adult diapers. (HENRY: Um—) Want kids? Can't have 'em with her.

HENRY: It's only been a couple of weeks . . .

ANNA: And you're already meeting her *family*! And of *course* you'll want a kid—every man wants a "mini him" to pass / things down to—

HENRY: Well, I'll just have them with you then. Keep it in the family. *(beat)* I'm KIDDING. I was looking forward to meeting you, you know. She said you were amazing.

ANNA: Well, here I am, in all my amazing glory, and *(getting up)* it was nice to meet you, my slutty mother's underage boy toy.

HENRY: You know, you shouldn't talk about her like that—

ANNA: I'm talking about you, *American Gigolo.*

HENRY: Well, she's *definitely* not *paying* me!

ANNA: Oh, that's good. That's something.

HENRY: And *Pretty Woman*, please, if I have to be a prostitute. I love that movie.

ANNA: Me too.

HENRY: And what would I even charge, three hundred bucks a night, like Julia?

ANNA: *(trying not to laugh)* Well, that was the '90s. You have to adjust for inflation.

HENRY: Oh, I did. I just figured Julia Roberts in the '90s is worth three times as much as I am now. *(ANNA laughs.)* Woah. Don't laugh at my dumb '90s joke! You might accidentally like me.

ANNA: Yeah, I might . . . accidentally like you already.

HENRY: Well, will you stay then?

ANNA: *(sitting back down)* I would have stayed for two thousand.

HENRY: I would have paid four.

ANNA: Hah. Because of / the movie.

HENRY: The movie.

ANNA: Or, you know, we could just get out of here—feels like we're really hitting it off—make some babies. *(beat)* Oh, look at your face! Now *I'm* kidding. I'm kidding.

HENRY: That was good. Friends?

Beat.

ANNA: It's a little too soon to tell.

COP CHATS 3 / COTTAGE FOUND

Sandeson's. GEENA *is wiping down tables.*

RAPP: Hey, Geena, Detective Rapp. Carson was saying your daughter's working here too?

GEENA: Uh-huh.

RAPP: I think I heard her on a podcast. She was serving the guy we're looking for . . .

GEENA: Oh yeah?

RAPP: She working tonight?

GEENA: Why, you wanna bust me for child labour?

RAPP: What? No. No . . . Just wanna put a face to a voice.

   CARSON *comes in.*

CARSON: Geena, two whiskies. Big ones!

GEENA: Whooo, party table.

RAPP: What's up?

CARSON: *(to* RAPP*)* We found it. The cabin in the frickin' woods.*

RAPP: Whaaa?

CARSON: *We checked out where your pal ol' Janice said she saw our favourite nudist, and about a mile from there we found a Pokémon hat in a *bush—*

RAPP: A Pokémon / hat—

CARSON: *(so excited)* Hat, yeah, that Mrs. Kalles said belonged to Henry, (RAPP: What?) and about half a mile from that we found this little wood cabin, (RAPP: Uh-huh.) a big fire pit out back (RAPP: No!) . . . and drum roll please . . . chickens! (RAPP: HAH!) Just a whole bunch a chickens! *And* guess what else? (RAPP: What?) A *sledgehammer*. Like in the podcast.

RAPP: A *sledgehammer*?

> GEENA *drops their drinks onto the table.*

CARSON: Thanks, Geena.

GEENA: Uh-huh.

RAPP: So—

CARSON: Forensics is sweeping for DNA—now we just have to wait for the lab, but holy shit.

RAPP: Holy shit. *(raises glass)* To dust for the chickens in the woods.

CARSON: Dust for the chickens in the woods. *(They drink.)* So you survived your dinner with the Boner Beast—any skeletons in her closet?

RAPP: She does have a mortar and pestle.

CARSON: Does she have a blender too?

> RAPP *laughs.*

RAPP: No, but she did tell me this crazy story about Ivan the Bold, and some horns, and a *phoenix.*

CARSON: *(rolls her eyes)* Did she say anything *useful?*

RAPP: She has an alibi for the sixteenth. And *if* the murder weapon is the sledgehammer, I'm not liking Elena for it . . . I don't think she could even *lift* a sledgehammer.

CARSON: Oh, right, so guess who owns the land?

RAPP: . . . Elena?

CARSON: Uh-uh. *Anna* Yazov.

RAPP: That's the daughter. (**CARSON:** What?) Oh, Katherine has a daughter.

CARSON: *What?*

RAPP: Geena, we're gonna need another round!

GEENA: *(off stage)* You got it.

CARSON: *(to RAPP)* Where's the *daughter?*

RAPP: Katherine says she lives in Europe.

CARSON: But she owns a cabin here?

RAPP: Yeah, and she knew Henry, or she met him. And Anna and Katherine are in some kind of a . . . fight or something, and Elena doesn't get along with her either. I haven't been able to get in touch with her . . .

CARSON: So maybe it's personal. Jealousy. Henry was sleeping with Katherine, he meets Anna. If Anna is anything like her mom . . .

RAPP: What does *that* mean?

CARSON: "*Witchy*" energy.

RAPP: Shut up.

CARSON: Maybe Henry developed a thing for the daughter. Maybe mom got jealous and killed . . . both of them?

RAPP: Or, Katherine mentioned she brought her mother to her last school too. I looked into it—ten years ago she was at Fletcher University, where some fuckboy named Luke Finnegan went missing and—get this—kid was an English major, writing a book. Guess what that book was about?

CARSON: No way.

RAPP: Baba fucking Yaga. They never found him. And three months later she got the job out here. Did you look into David Becker?

CARSON: Yeah, but didn't get much. He was a young guy—he was never found. His father filed the report but passed away a few years ago.

RAPP: I think these guys could be connected: David Becker, Luke Finnegan, Henry. Elena was in Fletcher too, with Katherine. Now they're here. Maybe . . . they do it together. Maybe they're some kind of . . . like, serial-killing mother-daughter duo . . .

CARSON: *(laughing)* We still don't have a body! *Any* body!

RAPP: Geena, same again, please.

GEENA: *(off stage)* Okay.

RAPP: Or, Elena said "she must always be three." In some stories Baba Yaga is three women—usually sisters, but it could be generational . . .

CARSON: Okay, but if Anna lives in Europe, does she commute in on her broomstick?

RAPP: *(having fun, acknowledging it's crazy)* No, I'm not saying . . . Okay, just go with me on this, maybe the Yazovs are obsessed with Baba Yaga. Maybe they make their victims obsessed too . . . the podcast, the book. But how?

GEENA enters with the bottle.

CARSON: Magic!

RAPP: So what's their type? Rich young men?

CARSON: David Becker worked in a gas station.

RAPP: Dumb young men?

GEENA: *(pouring)* I know a few of those.

RAPP: *(to CARSON)* Come on! Gimme a theory!

CARSON: Okay, you said Luke Finnegan was a fuckboy?

RAPP: Uh-huh. Seems like he ploughed his way through the Fletcher undergrads.

CARSON: Okay, Henry got around too, right? That's what Pam Riley said?

RAPP: Okay, I see where you're going! It is always the slutty ones that get murdered in the movies. So, maybe they target—

CARSON: Loose men?

RAPP: "Loose"?

CARSON: Yes, loose.

RAPP: Okay, well, maybe that's what made Henry a "bad dog." That's what made David Becker a POFS.

CARSON: POFS?

RAPP: Piece of fucking shit—"cheat on your woman, you get the hammer."

CARSON: Is *that* a Baba Yaga thing?

RAPP: Nah, she mostly eats kids.

CARSON: *(finding this funny)* Well, maybe that's what she used to do, but this is a Baba Yaga for the twenty-first century, lying in wait in the woods for loose men, fighting fuckboys with magic! And this time she has help.

RAPP: One more, Geena!

GEENA: *(off stage)* Uh-huh.

RAPP: You think this is funny. *(joking)* This is a real, serious investigative theory.

CARSON: I . . . *(giggling)* no, I just think it's unlikely.

RAPP: Okay, "loose men."

GEENA *comes on with the bottle. Pours for them.*

CARSON: Shut up.

RAPP: But "loose" doesn't seem like enough, you know? You guys, women, you need to have, like, a *reason* to murder.

GEENA: *(pouring)* Oh, yeah? Do we?

GEENA *goes.*

CARSON: Well, it would be nice if it was true, your theory.

RAPP: Nice? I guess it would be nice. A nice break from the losers in white vans who kidnap girls and wear their faces and say they were asking for it.

CARSON: Geez, that's who you'd kill, huh, losers in white vans?

RAPP: Maybe, if I was going to . . . I certainly wouldn't do it with my MOM. GEENA!

RAPP laughs.

CARSON: Can you imagine? She'd be like . . . *(funny voice)* Did you buy bleach?

RAPP: You're driving too fast!

CARSON: Are you *sure* you wouldn't rather just have a baby?

GEENA comes on with the bottle again.

Woah. Did I just get drunk? I'm drunk.

GEENA: *(to RAPP)* You might want to slow down.

RAPP: TELL IT TO THE COWS, YOU MURDERER.

GEENA: Yep, you're cut off.

RAPP: Geena. Geena!

GEENA goes.

CARSON: It's okay, I'm *done.*

RAPP: No, no! Come on! There's no one to hang out with in this fucking town!

CARSON: What about your sexy professor?

RAPP: That was just *collecting intel.*

CARSON: Right.

RAPP: So you want to have a baby?

CARSON: *(chokes a little on her drink)* Oh . . . Not right now, thanks. Do *you* have kids?

RAPP: Not that I know of. (**CARSON:** Ugh.) Come on, I'm a low-key alcoholic and I'm obsessed with work . . . Do you think I could find someone who could stand me long enough to want my offspring?

CARSON: Absolutely not.

RAPP: Exactly. Do you? Want a baby. Not *mine.*

CARSON: I don't know. I guess it would depend on my partner.

RAPP: Oh, you have a partner? Like not a police partner?

CARSON: No, no.

RAPP: How come?

Beat.

CARSON: I have kind of a hard time . . . trusting people.

RAPP: You don't say.

CARSON: Shut up. And . . . I . . . *love* my job and it keeps me really busy.

RAPP: Yeah. Uh-huh. *(beat)* What made you want to be a cop?

CARSON: You know. Standard dad cop stuff.

RAPP: Your dad was a cop?

CARSON: Uh-huh. Right here in Whittock. What made you want to be a cop and *settle* for being a PI?

RAPP: Hah. I guess . . . *(earnest)* I've always really liked puzzles. Finding things. Answers.

CARSON: Wow, you're a walking detective cliché.

RAPP: I know. *(laughs)* But I'm good at it. You're good too, I think.

CARSON: No I'm not. I didn't make any headway on Henry till you showed up.

RAPP: Okay, well, you're a good person. I knew it when you drank the coffee.

CARSON: What are you talking about?

RAPP: If I can, when I meet a new person, I always offer to buy them a coffee, and then get it wrong. It's a *tactic*—I do it on purpose.

CARSON: A *tactic*.

RAPP: Yeah, when you give a person a thing they don't want, you get to see what kind of a person they are, how they react. Three kinds of people—the kind that doesn't drink it, the kind that makes you get a new one, and the kind that drinks it because they don't want you to feel bad. Good person.

CARSON: That's . . . so *stupid!*

RAPP: Nah, you gotta try it.

They're very close, almost touching. CARSON *is awkward.*

CARSON: Yeah, *(downs energy drink)* I'm going to wake up and go through these notes. See if we've missed something. *(on her way out)* Hey, you messed up! You didn't offer Elena a coffee!

CARSON goes.

RAPP: No . . . *(looking at bottle)* GEENA!

GEENA: Yeah?

RAPP: Can I get a burger to go?

GEENA: Please!

RAPP: Please.

ELENA 2

The hospital. RAPP *enters, a bit drunk, with a bottle of vodka and a Sandeson's Diner takeout bag.* ELENA *can be there already or enters after* RAPP.

RAPP: Elena? Dobrenday. *[Good day.]*

ELENA: *(correcting, but pleased)* Dobrenychy. *[Good evening.]*

He helps her sit down.

RAPP: Okay . . . You wanted my'aso—meat—so there's a burger in there—from Sandeson's . . . and . . . vodka . . .

Her eyes light up.

ELENA: Ohhhh! You are good boy. Good dog.

RAPP: You know, I *am* a good dog. Everyone says so.

ELENA: Don't forget to ask, when it is time.

RAPP: For what?

ELENA: The horns.

RAPP: *(humouring her)* Yeah, okay.

ELENA: Okay. *(takes a big drink, offers it to him).* Pyi! *[Drink up!]*

RAPP: Oh, I've . . . had some . . . okay. Pyi! And I know you wanted kvity— flowers . . . but it was late . . . but, looks like someone already brought you some! Where are those from?

ELENA: Onutsia. Do pobachennia. *[Goodbye.]* Is almost time.

RAPP: Onutsia—granddaughter? (**ELENA:** Mmm.) Anna . . . brought you those.

ELENA: Clever.

RAPP: *(getting up)* Is she here? Where is she?

ELENA: Kray svitu. The edge of the world . . . *(suddenly realizing he's alone)* Where is other one?

RAPP: Carson? Oh she's / working—

ELENA: You *like* her? You like her. You like her *(makes breast gesture)* hrudy.

RAPP: Oh! Hah! I mean, sure, she's . . . I mean, she looks nice.

ELENA: You like hrudy!

RAPP: Hey, hah, ho, I understand, but we're co-workers. I *respect* her . . . hrudy.

ELENA: Good dog.

They pass vodka back and forth. He takes a big drink.

RAPP: Elena . . . (**ELENA:** Hm?) We found Anna's cabin. And the hammer.

ELENA: Doesn't matter. Night is coming. Soon there will be dytia.

RAPP: That's . . . baby, right? Who's having a baby?

Beat.

ELENA: ME! *(laughs, wheezes)* No, no, molodsha! Me, I think I'm a little bit *too old.* But we could try . . .

RAPP: The youngest is having a baby? Anna? You said it's *her* job to kill the bad dog. Did she do it with Katherine?

ELENA: Ni!

RAPP: Did she kill him with a sledgehammer?

ELENA: *Ni!*

RAPP: Is Anna Baba Yaga?

ELENA: Ni! *(suddenly very frustrated)* My vsy yaha! *[We are all Yaga!]* Argg. You never ask the right question.

Beat.

RAPP: Elena, *why* did she kill the dog?

ELENA: *(smiling)* Ahhh . . . "Khto pidtoptav kvitku, musyt' posadity novo."

RAPP: I don't know / what that—

ELENA: You step on flower, you should build a garden.

RAPP: Did the dog . . . step on your flower?

ELENA: *(sadly)* Not my kvitka . . . *(clutches the Sandeson's bag).* Iilaia. *[Lily.]*

RAPP: Iilaia.

HENRY AND LILY

HENRY's dorm room. LILY *enters holding a red cup, like from a university party. Sounds of a party in the hall outside. She's nervous.*

LILY: Henry?

HENRY: Lily! Hey! It's just in here. Sorry about the mess.

LILY: Is this where you record your podcast?

HENRY: Yeah, usually. You should be a guest!

LILY: Really? (**HENRY:** Yeah!) I don't know what I'd . . . talk about. I'm not like . . . an expert on anything.

HENRY: Well, I'd pick the topic. I'd pick the "Lady Death Dealer."

LILY: Right, cool. That'd be cool.

HENRY: Did you want another whisky?

LILY: Oh! No, I'm okay. I mostly just drink coolers . . .

HENRY: Well, we could do Elizabeth Báthory.

LILY: What?

HENRY: For your podcast episode.

LILY: Oh, cool! Yeah, she's so great.

HENRY: It's okay if you don't know who she is.

LILY: *(laughs sheepishly)* I don't know who she is.

HENRY: Oh, man, she's awesome, so . . . she's this seventeenth-century Hungarian countess—she went kinda nuts and started killing virgins—

LILY: Virgins?

HENRY: Yeah, A LOT of virgins, like six hundred, and drinking and bathing in their blood to stay young looking.

LILY: Gross.

HENRY: Yeah, super gross, but that would make this middle-aged woman, like, the most prolific serial killer ever.

LILY: So cool!

HENRY: Right? I mean, I feel like my mother would do that now.

LILY: What?

HENRY: Kill virgins to stay young.

LILY: Hah!

HENRY: Probably easier to *find* virgins in the seventeenth century.

LILY: Yeah. *(laughs, she's a bit dizzy)* Can I sit down for a sec?

HENRY: Yeah, yeah, sit, sit. So we could talk about *her* on your episode. She's a badass lady. You're a badass lady.

LILY: Yeah, but . . . what would I say . . . about her? I'm not like . . . an expert on . . . countesses.

HENRY: Hah, no, but . . . you're a virgin, right?

Beat. LILY *laughs awkwardly.*

LILY: I . . .

HENRY: I'm totally kidding. I know you're not a virgin!

LILY: Yeah, / no . . .

HENRY: Totally.

LILY: No . . . *(beat, gets up to go)* I think I should go, maybe.

HENRY: *(grabbing her hand)* No, you have to see it . . . you came here to see it.

LILY: I . . . I've seen a lizard before. It's okay. I / should—

HENRY: No, it's so cool. It's growing its tail back . . . It'll take *two* seconds. Then we can go back to the party. *(holds her wrist)* Okay? *(beat)* Okay?

LILY

The alley outside of Sandeson's. GEENA *brings a bag of trash out.*

RAPP: Geena.

GEENA: What are you /. doing out here?

RAPP: Did you send me that tape? Henry's podcast with Katherine? Lily was there. Did you want me to look into it?

GEENA: What are you talking about?

RAPP: I know she knew Henry. I want to talk to her.

GEENA: Well, you can't. You think I'm stupid?

RAPP: No.

GEENA: This a test?

RAPP: What? No, Pam Riley said . . .

GEENA: Pam Riley . . . that little shit. She said she wouldn't tell anyone. Who else did she tell? Huh? Because they'll sue us, they'll fucking sue us!

RAPP: No one, nobody / knows anything.

GEENA: You police?

RAPP: No.

GEENA: I see you with Carson all the time.

RAPP: We're working together. Geena, do you know where Henry Kalles is?

GEENA: Why, you think I hurt him?

RAPP: You stabbed someone with tongs.

GEENA: You know Lily's fifteen? She's *fifteen*.

RAPP: She and Henry . . . had a . . . relationship?

GEENA: Relationship . . . hah. She thought he was cute. She'd always ask to serve him. He talked to her like a grown-up. Then one day he invited her to a party, on campus.

RAPP: You let her go?

GEENA: No! You got kids?

RAPP: No.

Beat.

GEENA: Doesn't matter what you say or do. You can't protect them. All you can do is clean up after.

Beat.

RAPP: So, she went to campus . . .

GEENA: He got her drunk, said he wanted to show her something in his room. A lizard or, fuck . . . I don't know. It was a month after it happened when she told me. She missed her period. She was scared shitless, broke down while we were . . . *(this is hard for her)* polishing cutlery. She just kept saying . . . "I'm smart. I'm a smart person, I knew what I was doing." Broke my fucking heart, cuz she is—she's smart, she's really fucking smart, but she's *fifteen*.

RAPP: And Pam Riley?

GEENA: Henry—that piece of shit brought her here. On a *date*. He kept bringing people in here, after it all happened. He'd order beers and burgers from Lily like he'd never met her—why the fuck would he do that? When he brought Pam . . . my Lily, she just started shaking, crying. I watched Lily follow Pam into the bathroom and she just . . . told her everything.

RAPP: Why?

GEENA: *(emotional)* She said . . . she said she wanted her to *know*. She said girls should know about guys who do that. "Girls should know not to be with guys like that," she said. *She* wanted to protect *Pam*—so she told her what had happened, and Pam promised not to tell.

RAPP: Did Pam tell her to go to the witch?

GEENA: *(resolved)* I took her to the witch. Doctor would have talked, and they said they'd sue us. They would have taken the diner. So we settled.

RAPP: Settled? With who?

GEENA: Who the fuck do you think?

RAPP: Mrs. Kalles. Jesus, you must have been mad as hell. Threats from the mother then watching him bring dates through Sandeson's. Did you do something to him, Geena? What did you do?

Beat.

GEENA: Don't *you* know?

I GET IT NOW

CARSON's office. CARSON is holding some papers when RAPP storms in.

CARSON: I was just gonna call you! Everything came back from the lab—bone fragments in the soil and fire pit, brain tissue on the sledgehammer . . . It's Henry. And there's / something else—

RAPP: I spoke to Geena last night.

Beat.

CARSON: Why / did you—

RAPP: No, no, why don't YOU tell ME why I was talking to Geena? "Don't you know?" she said, which makes me look like an idiot, (**CARSON:** Rapp.) and I get it, I really do—why you were doing such a shitty job of looking for Henry before I came along, because Geena said she went to the *police.*

CARSON: I *was* going to tell / you . . .

RAPP: You don't think maybe that's *motive*? You knew what Henry did to Lily—you've known this whole time—and can't think why / for the life of me—

CARSON: The Kalles lawyers shut the whole thing down. No witnesses, too late for a rape kit, and to top it off, they said, "Why would a guy like Henry need to rape an *ugly* fifteen-year-old *townie*?" *(beat)* Everyone signed NDAS, all my higher-ups got hush money, and I didn't get a choice.

Beat.

RAPP: That's terrible, but what you think you're doing? Some kind of reverse vigilante justice here trying to not look for Henry? (**CARSON:** I am—) You don't think it matters he's ground to dust?*

CARSON: Of course—

RAPP: *I don't want to tell you how to do your job . . .

CARSON: Then don't.

RAPP: THEN DO IT.

CARSON: Your job's done. You found him! He's dead—take your money and go home!

RAPP: You know I honestly thought you were a good person. A good cop.

CARSON: BECAUSE OF THE COFFEE? (**RAPP:** Fuck off.) Rapp. I *babysat* Lily Sandeson and *she's* a good person. A good kid. And now that's going to be part of her forever, and the people who were supposed to help her, we just swept it under the rug. Now, at least Henry can't do that to anyone else.

   Beat.

RAPP: I'm sorry that happened to your friend. I am. But you can't say that he deserved to die. That's not your call. You can't just sweep Henry under a rug / because—

CARSON: He belongs under a rug! He should be dust. (*She's emotional.*) (**RAPP:** Carson.) No, I'm fine. It just made me feel . . . I'm sorry I didn't tell you. I couldn't. But now it's bigger. They found other bones. Fragments. At the cabin. From more than one person.

RAPP: I fucking knew it.

CARSON: Look, we don't get stuff like this out here in Whittock. I . . .

RAPP: I'm still here. Let's figure it out. Henry and Lily. *That's* motive. For who?

CARSON: I . . . Geena. Maybe Lily. Elena knew about it. But I / don't think—

RAPP: No, we know the Yazovs are involved—the bones, the cabin, Baba Yaga. Elena said "we are all Yaga." Maybe *together* the Yazovs are Baba Yaga. They think they are. (**CARSON:** Okay.) They're killing according to a code, bad dogs. They're like a vigilante cult / who—

CARSON: Baba Yaga isn't EVIDENCE. A *real* person killed Henry with a sledgehammer, so let's talk about *real* people! Geena, Lily, the Yazovs, but Katherine has an alibi, Elena can't lift a sledgehammer, Anna is in Europe.

RAPP: No she's not! She was at the hospital last night to see Elena.

CARSON: So she's *here*?

RAPP: Katherine said Anna met Henry on a visit. Two visits in a month? What if Katherine's lying about Anna living in Europe?

CARSON: If Anna is here, she could be the one Janice saw in the woods.

RAPP: But if she lives here, and she knows Henry, then why haven't we talked to her?

CARSON: Because she doesn't want to talk to us.

RAPP: Maybe we're asking the wrong questions. It's not where Anna is, it's *who*. She could be someone we've talked to.

CARSON: But why would Anna *help* us? Point us toward her family?

RAPP: I don't know.

CARSON: You said they were fighting, right? Katherine, Anna . . . you said Elena didn't get along with her either. Maybe she wants *them* to get caught. Maybe it is personal. Maybe *Anna* sent you that file.

RAPP: But what about the baby?

CARSON: What *baby*?

RAPP: There's supposed to be a baby! Night is coming, Elena is about to die . . . she said the youngest is pregnant.

CARSON: And . . . *if* Anna *is* pregnant . . .

RAPP: She'd be someone . . .

CARSON: Younger . . .

RAPP: Someone who could lift a sledgehammer. Someone strong. Someone angry.

CARSON: With a link to the Yazovs. Who has a problem with Katherine.

RAPP: Someone who knew Henry. And hates him. Someone violent.

Beat. They look at each other.

CARSON: We have to talk to Pam Riley.

THREE OF US

YAGA: Three is a good number.
Three wishes, three witches, three words.
Three parts of a story.
Three bears, three fates, three Stooges.
You can make *decisions* with three—you can get things DONE.
So, every so often, there must be a baby.
Now, we all have a say, but the youngest decides, it's her body—we only ask that she not take too fucking long.
First you have to find the man.
That sounds easy, but it's not, because there are so many men, and so many of them are stupid.
Stupid men make stupid babies.
And nobody wants a stupid baby.
So it is important that he is clever.
The other important thing is that he's handsome—being handsome doesn't make a better baby, but it doesn't hurt. Besides, we have to fuck him and that's more fun if he's good-looking, that's just the truth.
Now, how it works: the man is drawn to us. Pheromones, smell, how our hips sway: *magic.*
He devours us with his eyes, breathes us in, and imagines fucking us with his very soul.
As for the fucking, I don't have to tell you about it.
It's very good.
We are *fantastic* in bed. Sometimes we throw in tricks, we have a nice time.
Once is enough, for the baby. But sometimes we do it more. If we want.
Me, I always want. So sue me, it's fun.
And of course, there are magic words.
And let me tell you, magic is fucking hard.
But a baby is magic, so it's worth it:

Without her, there can be no beginning, no middle, no end.
So there must be three because three is forever.
And timing . . . is everything:
You can't fight time. It always runs out.
Tick tock.

INTERROGATION

The police station. KATHERINE *sits alone at a table.* RAPP *watches through a two-way mirror.* CARSON *comes in with a cup of coffee and puts it in front of* KATHERINE. CARSON *drinks a diet Red Bull.*

CARSON: Sugar, right?

KATHERINE: No.

CARSON: Oh . . . *

KATHERINE: Black.

CARSON: *Shoot. Want me to go get you another one?

KATHERINE: Yes, please, would you?

Beat. CARSON *smiles.*

CARSON: You know what, I actually think that was the last of the coffee. Sorry.

KATHERINE: Huh. Where's Detective Rapp?

CARSON: Well, as a private investigator, he's not able to sit in on official police business.

KATHERINE: Oh. I thought he was—

CARSON: What?

KATHERINE: Is he watching? *(looking at mirror)* He's watching, isn't he? Through there?

CARSON: *(looking)* That's a mirror.

KATHERINE: Give me some credit—I watch television.

CARSON: Then you know about mirrors . . .

KATHERINE: *(looking around)* I'm surprised this particular police department has the capacity for equipment like *(gestures to mirror)* that.

CARSON: A wall?

KATHERINE: So he'll be watching the interrogation?

CARSON: Oh, it's just a conversation . . .

KATHERINE: Until someone says the wrong thing.

CARSON: He said you were smart.

KATHERINE: He said you were pretty.

CARSON: Two doctorates. Should I call you *Doctor Doctor* Yazov then?

KATHERINE: No. What should I call you?

CARSON: Detective Carson.

KATHERINE: Are *you* a real detective?

CARSON: Of course. I have a badge and everything. (KATHERINE: Of course.) You could have asked to see *his* badge. Or maybe you were . . . distracted?

KATHERINE: You know, you sound a bit jealous.

CARSON: Pardon?

KATHERINE: I take it you haven't had the pleasure of being distracted by Mr. Rapp. He's *very* inventive.*

CARSON: Inventive.

KATHERINE: *Or maybe you just haven't piqued his interest—he did say you were a bit *(looking at mirror)* . . . was it . . . *tight*?

CARSON looks at the mirror too, knowing RAPP is there.

CARSON: Oh. Tight.

KATHERINE: Yes, tight.

CARSON: *(recovering)* You know, I've never met someone with two doctorates.

KATHERINE: I've never met a lady detective before.

CARSON: A *"lady* / detective"?

KATHERINE: I've only seen them on TV. (**CARSON:** Ah.) There's that television show about that group of women detectives who have a difficult time balancing work and home life— *(TV voice)* "How will they ever catch the killer *and* get dinner on the table for the kids. LADYCOPS." *(CARSON laughs.)* How do you do it?

CARSON: Don't have kids.

KATHERINE: Oh, I'm sorry.

CARSON: I'll be okay.

KATHERINE: Tick tock.

CARSON: Hah. / Wow.

KATHERINE: Then again, I can't imagine it's very safe, your line of work. Bad for parenting. And it must be very physical.

CARSON: Physical?

KATHERINE: Physically demanding if you have to . . . overpower someone stronger?

CARSON: Well, *I* have a gun but how would *you* do it?

KATHERINE: Why would I need to?

CARSON: How would you get rid of the body?*

KATHERINE: I'm sorry?

CARSON: *Would you grind up the bones?

KATHERINE: Honestly, if this / is about Baba Yaga—

CARSON: I'm sorry, I'm getting ahead of myself, / I should—

KATHERINE: May I see *your* badge?

CARSON: Sure.

    CARSON shows her badge.

KATHERINE: How do I know *that's* real?

CARSON: Well, you're being detained in a police station . . .

KATHERINE: Detained? I thought this was just a conversation.

CARSON: You were offered a lawyer when they brought you in. You didn't want one?

KATHERINE: Well, am I being detained or *arrested*?

CARSON: That depends on what you say about Henry.

KATHERINE: Look, I've been very co-operative. I came down here of my own free will when you called. I don't know where Henry is—I wish I did.

CARSON: Well that's okay, we've found him.

KATHERINE: You have?

CARSON: Yeah.

KATHERINE: *(worried)* . . . Well, is he all right?

CARSON: Oh, no, no. He's dead. Are you okay to keep going?

Beat.

KATHERINE: How . . . / did he—

CARSON: It's just difficult to tell, because we only have his bones. Bits of bone.

KATHERINE: Bits.

CARSON: It's like dust. Bone dust. All mixed in with dirt and a little bit of chicken shit outside in the garden at your cottage. *(beat, gauges KATHERINE's reaction)* It's a *beautiful* garden. Gorgeous perennials.

KATHERINE: It's . . . not *mine*.

CARSON: Right. It's your daughter's—Anna's?

Beat.

KATHERINE: How do you know they're Henry's bones?

CARSON: What an odd thing to say.

KATHERINE: It's just that it's almost impossible to get DNA from ground-up, burnt bone fragments.

CARSON: Well, we have a very good lab . . . Did I say they were burnt?

Beat.

KATHERINE: Detective—

CARSON: What do you think about the sledgehammer? (KATHERINE: Uh—) We're pretty sure that's what killed Henry, but isn't that what you said *Baba Yaga* might have done? Bludgeon a guy to death with a sledgehammer, burn his body, grind up the bones, use them as fertilizer . . .

KATHERINE: That was / *a podcast*—

CARSON: But that's CRAZY, you're *a* smart person—two doctorates—and it wouldn't be very smart to kill someone in EXACTLY the way you describe on a podcast, would it . . .

KATHERINE: No, / if—

CARSON: And how WOULD you grind up the bones, anyway—*

KATHERINE: I . . .

CARSON: *You COULD do it with a mortar and pestle, if you *had* to. Like the big one Rapp says you have one.

KATHERINE: For goodness/ sakes.

CARSON: Though it would probably take *forever*. Unless you had help.

KATHERINE: This is *ridiculous.*

CARSON: I don't know, *you* had an alibi for the sixteenth, and I don't think your mother could bludgeon anyone with a sledgehammer . . . but your daughter could, maybe. So where is Anna?

Beat.

KATHERINE: Like I told Mr. Detective, she's in Europe.

CARSON: There's no point, Katherine. We know Anna visited Elena in the hospital last night.

KATHERINE: What?

CARSON: And we know about Henry.

KATHERINE: You know he's dead—that's all you know.

CARSON: Well, I'd like you to explain it to me.

KATHERINE: Well, I'd like to be forty again.

CARSON: *(laughs)* Okay. Here's what I think. I think you're telling the truth—you didn't kill Henry. *(KATHERINE stands to leave.)* Geena brought Lily to Elena, and that's when you chose Henry as your victim. Sit down, please. *(KATHERINE sits.)* You started sleeping with him, introduced him to your daughter, but they started something up—I don't know if that's part of the plan, but *she* took him to the cottage and bludgeoned him, in the same way you described on the podcast, maybe to incriminate you, maybe because that's how you always do it, (KATHERINE: Always?) and then some combo of the three of you burnt his body and ground up his bones, then used his credit card to purchase a ticket to Prague / as a—

KATHERINE: Is this what Mr. Detective thinks?

CARSON: Oh, Rapp also thinks you're waiting for a magical baby and that you're a cult of vigilante witches, (**KATHERINE:** Really?) and, honestly, if that's the case, AWESOME, but either way . . . I think Anna is in Whittock and has been for a long time.

KATHERINE: Why would you think that?

CARSON: Parents like to keep their children close, isn't that right? She was even in your *class*. (**KATHERINE:** What?) She had a relationship with Henry and doesn't like him very much. She clearly has an axe to grind with her family because she's the one that told us to look into you and your mother. She's angry, she's strong, and she has a mean right hook.

KATHERINE: Who are you talking / about—

CARSON: So we went to Pam Riley's dorm room—she wasn't there—but we did find this.

CARSON pulls out a small photograph and slams it down on the table in front of KATHERINE.

That's you, right? (*KATHERINE ignores it.*) You want to tell me why a student, who *hates you*, right, because you failed her—has a picture of you holding a baby? (*KATHERINE snatches at the photo.*) My guess is that's baby Anna . . . or Pam. I think they're the same person, and I think when we arrest Pam Riley, or Anna Yazov, she's going to have a lot to answer for. I'm sorry, did you want another coffee?

KATHERINE: (*beat, hard*) No, I want my lawyer.

LET'S GO TO PRAGUE

A motel room. *HENRY is wearing his Pokémon hat.*

ANNA: Hi.

HENRY: Hey. Come here.

ANNA: This room is *awful.*

HENRY: You said not on campus. Come here.

ANNA: Henry, wait.

HENRY: What?

ANNA: My mom cannot find out.

HENRY: That was the whole point of getting the room.

ANNA: You thought *this* room would make me finally sleep with you?

HENRY: Well, let's do that right / now!

ANNA: No, no. It should be like *Pretty Woman*, not *Psycho*. (**HENRY:** Hah!) I want it to be special when we do.

HENRY: *(gesturing between them)* This *is* special. Tell me you don't feel this. *Electricity.*

ANNA: No, no. There's like a smell in here. I think for the time being you'll have to be content with my wrinkly boring old mom.

HENRY: *She's* not boring.

ANNA: Please, I've taken her class.

HENRY: That's not what I meant. (**ANNA:** Ugh.) Hey, hey, you're perfect.

ANNA: *(softening)* Thank you.

HENRY: Stay and have a drink.

ANNA: Oh, I actually brought . . .

She pulls out a bottle of something dubious.

HENRY: *(sniffs it) Oof.* What is that?

ANNA: Ukrainian moonshine.

They drink from the bottle. It's strong.

Molotok. My grandma makes it from like, roots—she says it keeps her young, but mostly it just gets you / really drunk.

HENRY: *(kissing her)* Come away with me.

ANNA: *(laughing)* What?

HENRY: For real! Let me be your Richard Gere. *(laughs)* Let me take you away! Money's not an issue, we can go anywhere you want! London. Paris. *Prague.*

ANNA: Do you want to go somewhere real?

HENRY: Where?

ANNA: Our family cottage. It's like an hour away. We could spend the night. It's really . . . special.

HENRY: Fuck yeah, let's spend a night in a cabin in the woods! But up there, all alone . . . I mean, I'm *definitely* gonna try to sleep with you.

ANNA: I mean that's kind of the point. And I think I can handle you.

VICTORY

RAPP's motel room. RAPP is drinking.

RAPP: Hey, you came to see me off. Want a drink? Toast to a job well done?

He pours some into two plastic-wrapped cups.

CARSON: Not quite done yet. Still looking for Pam.

RAPP: Or . . . just to say goodbye then. (**CARSON:** Goodbye?) I'm leaving in the morning. (**CARSON:** Oh.) I'm gonna go collect my yoghurt blood money and disappear for a bit. Take a break from the losers in white vans, you know? And the witches. But *you* don't think they're witches.

CARSON: No. But I . . . spoke to Pam's coach. She said Pam was pregnant. (**RAPP:** Oh *shit!*) So *you* don't think you're crazy. Even though I still do.

RAPP: Thank you. You know, you were pretty amazing in there.

CARSON: Thank you.

RAPP: Told you you were a good cop.

CARSON: Hah. She's a piece of work, Katherine.

RAPP: Yeah. I'm sorry I told her you were . . . tight.

CARSON: I've been called worse by worse people than your witchy *girlfriend.*

RAPP: Shaddup.

CARSON: Well, you slept with her, didn't you?

RAPP: What?

CARSON: Yeah, it's fine, intel, whatever. It worked. Thank you for fucking her, partner.

RAPP: What? Are you kidding? I didn't *sleep* with her!

CARSON: She said . . .

RAPP: NO! She said all that to fuck with *you*, and clearly . . . *(beat)* Okay. Wow.

CARSON: Shut up.

RAPP: You *are* jealous!

CARSON: SHUT UP. Okay, I'm going. It was nice . . . working with you. Two heads. Ugh.

RAPP: Um, stay. For a bit.

CARSON: For what?

RAPP: I dunno. We could . . . um, talk more about . . . the case. About witches . . . I could tell you about Ivan the Bold . . .

CARSON: Okay . . .

RAPP: Okay, here goes. Sit, sit. *(a bit drunk as he talks)* Once upon a time there was a handsome merchant's son, Ivan, who was looking for a beautiful princess.

CARSON: As usual.

RAPP: So he went to the chicken hut to ask Baba Yaga for help. Now, there's a bit of a routine that went on here. Baba Yaga would say, *(funny voice)* "Whew, what a smell, there must be a stinky Russian nearby." (**CARSON:** That's what she sounds like?) No, whatever. Then she'd ask, "Are you here because you want to be, or because you are *compelled*?"

CARSON: That like a consent thing?

RAPP: Kind of—and he'd say, "Mostly because I want to be, and even more because I'm *compelled*." Did she know where the princess was? "*Nah,*" she'd say, "But her *sister* might know." So he goes down the road to the sister and they do the whole bit again: Does she know where the princess is? Nope! So she directs him to the *third* Baba Yaga, but she warns him, "The youngest one *may* try to eat you, and if that happens, you ask her for the horns"—

CARSON: The *horns*.

RAPP: So he goes to the youngest and she tells *him* where the princess is, but then she's like, fuck it, I don't care about your princess, I'm for sure gonna eat you! *(dramatic, selling it)* But then . . . he remembers the *horns*! And he asks for them, and she *has* to give them to him, because those are, like, the weird Yaga rules, and he blows them, and a *great phoenix* comes . . . And Ivan flies away on the phoenix's back, and Baba Yaga is left all alone in the woods with a fistful of phoenix feathers. *(beat)* ISN'T THAT FUCKED?

CARSON: *(laughing)* Yes, it is. Why do you like it so much?

RAPP: Because it's fucking . . . it's so . . . *crazy*. But it's also kind of . . . beautiful? And sad. You know, because she does help him, but maybe she just wanted him to like . . . stay and talk to her . . . And he's just like . . . see ya, flying off on a phoenix to find my hot young bride and have a million babies. But maybe he would have stayed but she didn't know how to ask him because she was so used to being alone . . . in the woods

. . . that she never let herself because she has . . . trust issues . . . *(beat)* Anyway, I think it's really beautiful. And fucked up. Isn't it?

CARSON: *(looking at him)* Yeah. It kind of is.

Beat. They sit in silence.

RAPP: Do you want another drink?

CARSON: Is that a good idea?

RAPP: Probably not.

RAPP goes to kiss her. She pushes him off.

Sorry. Sorry. Fuck.

She kisses him back. Sexy makeouts. Maybe he picks her up and carries her off to the bed.

THE BOY (I SMELL HIM)

YAGA: I smell him as soon as he comes within a mile of the hut.
Sweat, sex, sweet red wine, leather, salt, delicious.
He sees the skulls on the fence and—
I ask my question: are you here because you want to be?
He wants to be here, but he feels compelled.
He knows what to say, he's *so* good at this.
He wants to know the same old, same old: Where's the kingdom? Where's the beautiful girl? Blah blah. Blah.
I tell him the usual: I don't know, but the next one might.
So he's off down the road to her to me to her, to me and—
I ask my question.
He wants to be here, he feels *compelled.*
Where is she, blah blah.
I tell him I don't know, but *she* might, the angry one.
And I tell him—about the horns.
I don't know why I tell him (he's cute, that's why).
Whose idea were the fucking horns anyways?
So he's off down the road to her to me to her to me, and this time the smell is . . . I can't.
I'm hungry, I want him—I want to eat him, I want to fuck him, I'm so hungry.
And he asks for—the horns.
The *fucking* HORNS.
What a joke— Can I blow your horns? Do you mind if I blow your horns?
And he puts his lips . . . I can almost taste him. I could lick his cheek—salt.
He blows the first one—*(makes a sound)* and the next one *(makes a louder sound)* and the last one *(makes a really loud sound).*
And that . . . BIRD comes.
That fucking bird.

He gets on its back, and I grab it, I grab at it, I grab its fucking tail, and I'm left with a handful of feathers and fire.
As. Usual!
And he's gone forever.

Until next time.

But I can still taste him.

SHE'S AT THE COTTAGE

RAPP's motel room. His cellphone rings on stage. He comes in, pulling on his shirt, answers the phone.

RAPP: Who is this?

KATHERINE stands on a different part of the stage, on the phone.

KATHERINE: Is that my favourite detective?

RAPP: Katherine?

CARSON comes on, in similar disarray.

CARSON: Who is it?

RAPP: *(to CARSON, whispered)* It's fucking Katherine Yazov.

CARSON: *(whispering)* What? Speakerphone! Put it on speaker!

RAPP puts it on speaker.

KATHERINE: Is that Lady Cop? Well done, Detective.

RAPP: *(to phone)* Where are you?

KATHERINE: The edge of the world, where the fire burns and the chickens bleed. At the hut in the trees, with teeth in its mouth.*

CARSON: *(mouthing)* How did she get out?

KATHERINE: *You wanted a witch, yes? Handcuffs, walls, and a sleepy guard should be the easiest thing to escape; Houdini could do it under-water, and he wasn't even a *woman*.

RAPP: Katherine, just stay there.

KATHERINE: Oh, we will. We're waiting for you. Babusia, dotsia, onutsia . . .

RAPP: Onutsia? Pam is there?

KATHERINE: Oh, she was *insistent* on coming. Mama's time is drawing to a close and she'd like to be sent off in the old way . . . although it isn't very pleasant. She wants me to burn her.

RAPP: Katherine, don't do anything. I'm coming to you.

KATHERINE: Just you. Don't bring the tight lady cop.

RAPP: Don't do anything stupid.

KATHERINE: How could I? I'm *very* smart.

Click—she hangs up.

RAPP: Tell me how to get there.

CARSON: No, I'm coming with you.

RAPP: No.

CARSON: I'll call for backup on the way.

RAPP: No cops.

CARSON: Rapp, you can't go alone.

RAPP: She said she'd kill her.

CARSON: She's not gonna kill her own mother, Rapp!

RAPP: *(looks at watch)* Jesus. It's three in the fucking morning.

CARSON *opens an energy drink from her bag and hands it to* RAPP.

CARSON: Here, you take this. I'll drive.

YAGA *appears.*

YAGA: So he's off down the road to her to me to her to me, and I can already smell him.

WOODS 1

They shift out of the motel and become ANNA *and* HENRY, *making their way through the woods on their way to the cabin with flashlights, drinking the molotok.*

ANNA: Henry. Henry, you doing okay?

HENRY: *(stumbling on something)* Shit! This is like a legit hike!

ANNA: Come on, Henry, enjoy the exercise before the exercise.

HENRY: How does your *grandmother* do this?

ANNA: The drinking helps.

HENRY: I bet.

She passes him the bottle. He swigs. He sees something in the distance.

Is that smoke?

ANNA: I don't see anything.

She takes his Pokémon hat off and kisses him hard. Then she throws it into the darkness.

HENRY: Fuck! I'll never find that!

ANNA: Ooops. Am I a bad girl?

HENRY: Yes.

ANNA: Are you going to punish me?

HENRY: *(woozy)* . . . Yes.

ANNA: *(running off)* You'll have to catch me first.

YAGA: So he's off down the road to her to me to her to me. I can almost taste him.

WOODS 2

CARSON and RAPP make their way through the same woods with flashlights. RAPP catches up to CARSON, breathing heavily. The air is smoky.

RAPP: Carson, Carson, wait up!

CARSON: It's just over there.

RAPP: Where?

CARSON: There. Can you see it?

RAPP: No. Fuck, I'm so hot.

He rests on something. CARSON sees something in the distance.

CARSON: There's smoke—why is there smoke?

RAPP: She said she would burn her . . . *(breathing so heavily now)* I can't / see anything.

CARSON: Did you hear that?

RAPP: Everything's . . . spinning.

YAGA: The smell . . .

CARSON: I think someone's out there.

RAPP: I just need to . . . / sit down—

CARSON: Rapp, are you okay? Rapp?

YAGA: I could almost lick his cheek.

CARSON: Someone's here.

YAGA: Poverny spynu do lisu i oblychchya do mene. *[Turn your back to the forest and your face to me.]*

MEET GRAN

ANNA and HENRY outside the cottage. We can hear the squawking of chickens, the sound of a fire. HENRY is also out of breath, spacey, drunk.

ANNA: Turn your back to the forest and your face to me.

HENRY: What did you say?

ANNA: I said we're here, Henry.

HENRY: *(looking around)* You didn't tell me there were chickens!

ANNA: Why, are you afraid of them? *(makes chicken sounds)* Chicken?

HENRY: Jesus, that fire is fucking . . . huge. What is that, brick?

ANNA: It's clay. Helps get the fire really hot.

HENRY: But who . . . lit it? We just / got here.

ANNA: Come on.

They go inside the cabin.

HENRY: Woah. Your grandma *built* this place? *(spacey)* Like . . . with her hands?

ANNA: Yeah, a long time ago. (**HENRY:** Cool.) Take off your clothes.

HENRY: You first.

ANNA: Nu-uh. My house, my rules. Take it all off. *(scary now)* I said OFF.

He takes his clothes off, down to his underwear. She takes them.

Do you like it when I'm in charge?

HENRY: Yeah.

ANNA: Then you're gonna love the next part.

HENRY: *(spacey, trying to take off his clothes)* Buttons are . . . hard . . .

ANNA: How are you feeling?

HENRY: A little drunk . . . sleepy.

ANNA: Sit down.

HENRY: That stuff is deadly.

She gets a chair and brings him over to it.

(dreamily) Are you going to do a little dance for me?

ANNA: Sort of . . .

He slumps in the chair.

You really do have a great body. It's a shame you're such a piece of shit.

HENRY: *(closing his eyes, drifting off)* Mmmm.

ANNA: What do you think, Baba?

ELENA emerges from the shadows holding a machete and a sledgehammer.

ELENA: Harne. *[Handsome.]*

ANNA: Where's the chicken?

ELENA: In a minute. Let me look at him! *(goes close to him)* Ivan . . . miy ostanniy Ivan. *[My last Ivan.]*

ANNA: *(a bit guiltily)* Ne Ivan.

ELENA: Anna!

ANNA: I'm sorry, I don't want this one.

ELENA: Vin povynen buty Ivanom! *[He must be Ivan!]*

ANNA: The next one, okay.

ELENA: There is no time! *(angry)* Ya khochu spaty! *[I want to sleep!]*

She was too loud. She wakes up HENRY, *who freaks out and scrambles to cover himself.*

HENRY: HOLY SHIT!

ANNA: *(to* ELENA*)* Why is he awake?

ELENA: Ty dav yomu molotok? *[Did you give him the hammer?]**

HENRY: Who is that?

ANNA: *Tak! Vin yoho vypyv! *[He drank it!]* It's not working!

HENRY: WHO IS THAT? Did you drug me?

ANNA: Calm down . . . it's just my grandma . . .

HENRY: *(getting up, dangerous)* YOUR GRANDMA?

ANNA: It's / okay—

HENRY: WHAT THE FUCK IS GOING ON?

ANNA: Nothing.

HENRY: Oh shit! *(sees* ELENA *approaching)* Holy fuck!

ELENA: Stiy netikai. *[You have to stay.]*

HENRY: You crazy fucking bitches!

> ELENA *blocks his path, but he pushes her aside.* ANNA *goes after him.*
> *They fight, he gets away.*

ANNA: *(going to* ELENA*)* Baba . . .

ELENA: *(terrifying)* Durne divcha, idy dobery yoho! *[Stupid girl, go get him!]*

ANNA: *(going after him)* Shit! Henry!

> *Blackout.*

THE HORNS

The cottage. RAPP *wakes up. He's in his underwear, sitting in a chair in the cabin. We hear the sounds of a raging fire. He's breathing heavily as he wakes.*

RAPP: What . . . Carson? CARSON!

KATHERINE: *(coming in with a large coil of rope)* I told you to come alone.

RAPP: Katherine, what did you do to her?

KATHERINE: You've been a very naughty boy.

RAPP: Where's Elena?

KATHERINE: Oh, she's still at the hospital, but she sends her regrets. She's *very* sorry to miss this.

RAPP: Why can't . . . I move . . .

KATHERINE: That's mama's molotok. Knocks you out like a hammer. Or it's *supposed* to . . . but she's been a little off her game. *(starts tying him to the chair)* Can't have you running off like young Henry.

RAPP: How did / you—

KATHERINE: You know, you must hear this all the time, but it's better if you don't talk. We just have to wait for the chicken.

RAPP: My clothes—

KATHERINE: Sometimes there are secret little metal bits; you know, buttons and tags that don't burn. I let you keep those though. *(of the underwear)* For modesty. Even though I've seen it all and . . . *(appreciative sound)* congratulations.

RAPP: What is this?

KATHERINE: Come on, you're supposed to be clever . . .

She grabs the sledgehammer.

RAPP: No. Please. Katherine . . .

CARSON comes in suddenly, gun drawn, pointed at KATHERINE.

CARSON: DROP THE WEAPON, YAZOV!

RAPP: Carson!

KATHERINE: Uh-oh, Lady Cop's here to rescue the prince from the wicked old witch?

CARSON: Yazov!

KATHERINE: Are you really gonna shoot me?

RAPP: Shoot her, Carson!

CARSON: DROP IT RIGHT NOW.

KATHERINE: But this is the best part.

CARSON: STEP AWAY FROM HIM.

KATHERINE turns to face her. She's beside RAPP, holding the sledgehammer.

KATHERINE: Think I can do it in one?*

RAPP: Carson!

CARSON: *Katherine!

RAPP: Shoot her, / Carson!

KATHERINE raises her arms as if she's about to cast a spell.

KATHERINE: Ya proklynayu / tebe do smerti! *[I curse you to death!]*

CARSON: Stop! / Stop!

RAPP: SHOOT HER, CARSON, SHOOT HER!

CARSON pulls the trigger. Click. It's empty. She and KATHERINE burst into laughter. CARSON lowers the gun.

CARSON: I couldn't catch the chicken.

KATHERINE: You're going to have to learn one of these days.

CARSON: What? I've never done it! Baba's usually here. You're supposed to do it now anyway . . .

RAPP: Carson?

KATHERINE: He's awake.

CARSON: Don't look at me, I gave him a double hit.

RAPP: Carson, / what the fuck—

KATHERINE: *(to RAPP)* Shh . . . Not now. / *(to CARSON)* You—

CARSON: Mom, can you just go get the chicken please? I'm really tired.

KATHERINE: I should hope so. Good night?

CARSON: Yes. Very productive.

KATHERINE: You made us wait long enough.

CARSON: Jesus, I'm sorry, I'm sorry! Chicken? Please?

KATHERINE: *(to RAPP)* The things we do for our children.

(to the chicken) Khody siu da! *[Come here!]*

> *KATHERINE goes, taking the machete, trying to coax a chicken.*

RAPP: *You're* Anna. You . . . killed Henry.

CARSON: *(valley girl)* OMG, are you a detective?

RAPP: Untie me right fucking now!

CARSON: Sorry, no.

RAPP: Pam—where the fuck is she?

CARSON: I don't know, probably at the gym.

RAPP: But . . . you grew up in Whittock.

CARSON: Oh yeah, with my cop dad, babysitting *poor* Lily.

RAPP: You do work for the police department.

CARSON: I've never taken a vacation. Lots of bad dogs.

RAPP: You sleep with them?

CARSON: No, no, unless I really want to. Mom always does, though. She loves it—she's prymanku, the lure, *very* skilled—as you know. Or . . . oh, but you didn't sleep with her, right? You didn't feel *compelled*?

RAPP: Okay, okay, I lied, but I'm not a bad dog!

CARSON: No, no, you were a lucky break—clever, handsome. *Affable*. My white knight. (**RAPP:** Jesus.) *(fake sad)* "I have trouble trusting people."

RAPP: Fuck you.

CARSON: Hey, I thought we both had fun and . . . *(puts her hand on her belly)* it was time for the baby, so . . .

RAPP: No. You slept with Henry, that's . . . / his—

CARSON: Ugh, no, never, that's why Gran was pissed—I cut it a little too close for her and mom. *(sound of a chicken off stage)* Call me millennial, I was holding out for something better for my Ivan, like you.

RAPP: No, you can't know / already—

CARSON: First time's a charm. The chicken just helps it stick, or gets rid of it, depending on what you want . . . And she'll be molotok *[hammer]*, and I'll be prymanku *[lure]*, and Mama will be lehenda *[legend]*, and the cycle goes on and on and on.

KATHERINE *comes in holding a dead chicken.*

KATHERINE: Durna kurka! *[Stupid bird!]* She bit me!

CARSON: Aw.

RAPP: This is fucking BULLSHIT—

KATHERINE: No, this is an *honour*. Begin.

CARSON beats the sledgehammer slowly, rhythmically against the floor. She and KATHERINE move in a circle around RAPP, with KATHERINE plucking and dropping the feathers in a circle around RAPP's chair, CARSON beating the sledgehammer.

RAPP: No! So what, you're just going to kill me too, burn my body and grind me up?

CARSON: It's going to take forever.

RAPP: No, stop doing that!

KATHERINE: Shh.

RAPP: People will look for me!

Another big hit of the sledgehammer—they reverse directions.

What do you want, money? I won't tell anyone what I know. You don't have to kill me.

KATHERINE: We don't need anything else from you.

CARSON: *(hand on her belly)* She's gonna be beautiful. Poverny spynu do lisu i oblychchya do mene. Poverny spynu do lisu i oblychchya do mene.

KATHERINE has finished plucking the feathers. CARSON readies herself behind RAPP's chair. KATHERINE dips her hands into the chicken and smears blood on RAPP's face and chest. CARSON holds the sledgehammer out for her. KATHERINE smears blood on its head. They chant rhythmically, building.

RAPP: No . . .

KATHERINE & CARSON: Poverny spynu do lisu i oblychchya do mene.

RAPP: Please.

CARSON: Poverny spynu do lisu i oblychchya do mene.

RAPP: Please.

Suddenly there are other women's voices, singing, or creating a scary soundscape. It grows louder, scary AF. Light shines from beneath the floorboards of the cabin.

KATHERINE & CARSON: Poverny spynu do lisu i oblychchya / do mene.

CARSON lifts the hammer, about to swing it at RAPP.

RAPP: No, no, I WANT THE HORNS.

The singing stops. Beat. CARSON lowers the sledgehammer.

CARSON: What? What did you say?

RAPP: The . . . horns! I want the horns! I'm asking for the horns.

CARSON looks at KATHERINE.

KATHERINE: I didn't think he'd remember.

CARSON: That fucking bird.

KATHERINE: Well. *(beat)* That's how it goes. Those are the rules. Give him the horns.

CARSON: Really??

KATHERINE: Yes.

RAPP: YES.

KATHERINE: You really want them?

RAPP: YES!

CARSON: Mom?

KATHERINE: Will you blow them?

RAPP: YES, I'LL BLOW THEM, I'LL BLOW THEM. I WANT THE HORNS, GIVE ME THE FUCKING HORNS.

Beat. The women look at each other. They're smiling.

KATHERINE: Detective, that only works in fairy tales.

The soundscape resumes. CARSON screams a battle cry and swings the sledgehammer. KATHERINE screams with her. RAPP screams. Blackout. Music. Soundscape. The blowing of horns, the beating of wings—escape on a giant fiery bird.

WHAT I TELL HER

ANNA: This is what I'll tell her.
The magic words are important.
Poverny spynu do lisu i oblychchya do mene.
Turn your back to the forest and your face to me.
Fly quickly, so no one can see you.
Use the pestle to steer, and a broom to cover your tracks.
Give him the drink, one swift blow to the head, *then* use the pestle.
You'll know when it's time for the baby.
But make your own choice, no matter what they say.
If he asks for the horns, give him the horns.
That doesn't mean you can't fuck with him first—just a little.
And remember, bad children are the softest, and the easiest to eat;
But a bad man's bones hold power, and power tastes like salt.
And salt is fucking delicious.
This is what I'll tell her.

   She goes.

And she will tell the next. And she will tell the next.

   RAPP emerges from the woods, shell-shocked, in a blanket. He can't see her.

Poof.

And then they were gone.

BLACK COFFEE

A clearing in the woods. RAPP *is in a blanket, shivering, shaking.*
SIDLE *comes in.*

SIDLE: Mr. Rapp, Staff Sergeant Lorna Sidle. My deputy said she was getting you some coffee. Bet you were cold . . . spending the whole night out here in the woods . . . but you know, with incidents like this—

RAPP: *(laughing a bit, trying to keep it together)* You get a lot of incidents like this?

SIDLE: Yes, son, indeed we do, and I know you boys don't point fingers, but what with all the chicken blood, I'm gonna guess this goes as far as hazing *and* animal cruelty . . .

RAPP: Hazing? No. No . . . You don't understand, they tied me up . . .

MURPHY: *(coming in with two coffees)* Okay, buddy, got your coffee—you said you wanted black?

RAPP: No.

MURPHY: Oh, shoot . . . I could get you another one?

Beat. He looks at MURPHY, *dismisses it.*

RAPP: No, listen . . . I'm a private investigator. I work for Mrs. Kalles. You were looking for her kid?

SIDLE: Yeah, last we decided the Kalles kid was in . . . / Prague?

RAPP: No, he's *dead!* The Yazovs killed him and ground his bones into dust, just like they did with David Becker and Luke Finnegan . . . Detective Carson—she's / in on it.

MURPHY: *(to SIDLE)* . . . Shirley?

RAPP: WHO THE FUCK IS SHIRLEY?

MURPHY: Shirley Carson's our receptionist.

RAPP: Receptionist? Well, can I talk to her?

MURPHY: She just went on vacation . . . but she's not a detective.

SIDLE: We don't have detectives out here. We're not that big a department.

RAPP: No, you have a lab! Forensics! They were out at the cabin, where you found me.

SIDLE: I don't know what you're talking 'bout, "forensics," "cabin"?

MURPHY: When I found you, you were out in the middle of the forest. No cabin, just you and a bunch of feathers . . .

RAPP: . . . Because it disappeared. (SIDLE: Oh?) Listen, Elena Yazov . . . the witch. She's in hospital . . .

SIDLE: Elena Yazov . . . died last night.

RAPP: *(starting to sound nuts, eureka!)* Because they have the baby now!

SIDLE: Yeah, I think maybe you just had a bit too much to drink . . .

MURPHY: Geena said you were a real handful a couple of nights ago at Sandeson's.

RAPP: GEENA KILLS CATTLE WITH A SLEDGEHAMMER! (**MURPHY:** Okay.) Is this . . . a joke? Is the whole fucking town in on it?

SIDLE: Now, now, son.

RAPP: *(picking up steam)* Okay, I know how this sounds, but the Yagas seduce and kill men and when the oldest gets too old, the youngest makes a baby with an Ivan—*I* am Ivan—and they *compelled* me, and *tricked me* into sleeping with them, and stole my sperm, and did the magic chicken ritual to make the baby stick, *(laughing a little maniacally)* and I'm only *alive* because I asked for the horns, and I blew the horns and the phoenix . . . came . . . I swear to God the phoenix came, but now my daughter's going to be a Yaga . . . Maybe YOU'RE Baba Yaga, maybe ALL WOMEN ARE BABA YAGA. Fuck!

SIDLE: Mr. Rapp, you've had a long night.

RAPP: You don't believe me. I get it. I wouldn't believe me either.

MURPHY: *(takes a sip of her coffee, spits)* Oh, this one's yours. I think I got 'em mixed up, buddy. Here. You want this one? Or are you afraid of cooties?

Beat. RAPP *looks at them in horror. No one will ever believe him.*

Beat.

RAPP: I'll drink it.

Blackout.

ACKNOWLEDGEMENTS

Thank you to everyone who helped bring this play off the page, onto the stage, and into this book, including Colleen Murphy, Jill Harper, Richard Rose, Joanna Falck, Tom McGee, Ann MacNaughton, Jerry Sandler, Seana McKenna, Claire Armstrong, Will Greenblatt, Rosemary Dunsmore, Allegra Fulton, Jesse LaVercombe, Noah Reid, Kat Letwin, Michael Musi, Claire Burns, Megan McCarthy, Carly Maga, Sarah Dodd, and the Feminist FUCK It Festival.

Kat Sandler is a playwright, director, screenwriter, and served as the artistic director of Theatre Brouhaha in Toronto. As a writer/director she has staged seventeen of her original plays in the past decade, including *Yaga* and the concurrent double bill of *The Party* and *The Candidate*, where the same cast raced back and forth between two theatres to perform two simultaneous plays. Her play *Mustard* won the Dora Mavor Moore Award for Best New Play and *Yaga* and *BANG BANG* were nominated for the same award. Kat is a graduate of the Queen's University Drama Program. She is based in Toronto, where she is still writing and directing plays and writing for television and film.